"Most youth workers feel like we just aren't reaching e̶ that's how I feel. In this book, Jonathan took me on a and encouraging at the same time! Instead of a few 'happy hops to heaven,' Jonathan provides a holistic approach to reaching this generation of unchurched students."

Kurt Johnston
Junior high pastor, Saddleback Church

"What a terrific book this is! More than a manifesto, it's a very practical guidebook on how to communicate the good news about Jesus to today's postmodern generation with love, grace, and humility."

Wayne Rice
Cofounder of Youth Specialties; director,
Understanding Your Teenager seminars

"This book is a biblically compelling and culturally relevant strategy for reaching today's unchurched teenagers for Christ. Many youth workers are either too quiet or too loud when it comes to telling the age-old gospel message to postmoderns, but Jonathan McKee strikes a refreshing balance that is much needed in today's youth ministry culture."

Greg Stier
Dare 2 Share Ministries

"This book is a treasure! Jonathan shows us that relational ministry to lost kids is compelling and doable for almost every follower of Christ. The book offers practical help for any Christian who wants to touch the life of a kid outside the family of God."

Jennifer Morgan
Senior director of campus ministry, Youth for Christ/USA

"You are holding in your hands a very practical, down-to-earth book on reaching unchurched students. I especially enjoyed the variety of stories that illustrated the points being made. It is obvious that Jonathan has a love of God and kids. What he is writing is real. It comes from hands-on experiences with youth. He knows kids, both churched and unchurched. He is no armchair strategist; he has been there. I think this would be a very valuable addition to any youth minister's library."

Les Christie
Professor of Youth Ministry, William Jessup University

If the statistic that 87 percent of people who become Christians make that commitment prior to age 21, then *Reaching Out To Unchurched Teenagers* should be required reading for youth workers. The good news: Jonathan doesn't just write about this . . . he does it. A decade ago I watched Jonathan start a campus ministry from nothing—no money, no staff, no facility, and no kids. Next thing you know, vanloads of *unchurched* kids are coming to church with him every week. Jonathan knows the unchurched, and he knows how to reach 'em.

Ray Johnston
Senior Pastor, Bayside Church
President, Developing Effective Leaders

DO THEY *RUN* WHEN THEY SEE YOU COMING?

REACHING OUT TO UNCHURCHED TEENAGERS

JONATHAN MCKEE

GRAND RAPIDS, MICHIGAN 49530 USA

www.youthspecialties.com

Do They Run When They See You Coming? Reaching Out to Unchurched Teenagers
Copyright © 2004 by Youth Specialties

Youth Specialties Products, 300 South Pierce Street, El Cajon, CA 92020 are published by
Zondervan, 5300 Patterson Avenue Southeast, Grand Rapids, MI 49530.

Library of Congress Cataloging-in-Publication Data

McKee, Jonathan R. (Jonathan Ray), 1970-
  Do they run when they see you coming? : reaching unchurched students
... without scaring them off! / by Jonathan McKee.
     p. cm.
  Includes bibliographical references and index.
  ISBN 0-310-25660-7 (softcover)
  1. Church work with students. 2. Church work with teenagers. 3.
Non-church-affiliated people. I. Title.
  BV4447.M237 2005
  259'.23--dc22

                                                                2004016914

Editorial direction by Dave Urbanski
Art direction by Jay Howver
Edited by Kevin Hendricks
Proofread by Laura Gross and Kristi Robison
Interior design by Holly Sharp
Cover design by Burnkit
Printed in the United States

---

05 06 07 08 09 /DC/ 10 9 8 7 6 5 4 3 2

TABLE OF CONTENTS

Acknowledgments

It is only by the grace of God that this book exists. My life has been full of many examples of how NOT to reach unchurched students. But by God's grace I've slowly learned from my mistakes, and now I'm passing a little of this knowledge on to others.

I thank my board at www.TheSourceForYouthMinistry.com for not only allowing me to work on this book, but also for uniting with me in our ministry to train youth leaders, to reach out to unchurched youth, and to provide free resources to youth workers across the world.

I couldn't have written this book without the years of mentoring I received from my good friend Leonard Lee. Leonard took me under his wing and taught me to look at kids differently. He taught me to let Christ's love flow through me. Leonard's teaching helped me develop parts of chapters 2 and 6. Leonard and I brainstormed chapter 8 together, and chapter 9 is a list of his questions. Leonard doesn't just teach others how to reach out to the unchurched—he does it.

I thank my father, Tom McKee, for his consistent help with this book. I don't think anyone else had to endure reading as many rewrites of this book as he did. And all the while, he encouraged me to press on.

I thank my wife, Lori, who not only put up with me during the writing of this book, but also proofed the whole thing from cover to cover. (Lori is the best proofreader I've seen. And she's all mine!)

Thanks to Gary Fox and Youth for Christ for giving me a start in full-time youth ministry and providing me the arena to reach out to the unchurched.

Jonathan McKee

Foreword

by Chap Clark

Over the years I have come to believe that few Christians recognize or are even aware of Peter's advice on sharing the gospel:

> "But in your hearts set apart Christ as Lord. Always be prepared to give an answer to everyone who asks you to give the reason for the hope that you have. But do this with gentleness and respect." (1 Peter 3:15)

Gentleness and respect—two words, or more importantly, two direct applications of love that are often lost in our zeal to confront those who do not know Christ with the truth of his love. In Galatians 5:22-23, the "fruit of the Spirit" passage, Paul similarly reminds us what the outcome (or fruit) of our walk with Jesus Christ should look like by using words such as *patience* and *kindness*. Again, God's prescription for us, even in our enthusiasm for those whom the Bible calls lost, when it comes to our approach toward them.

Gentleness...respect...patience...kindness.

Great words, these.

Perhaps God wants us to realize that it is he, by the strength of his love and the movement of his Spirit, who is the key player in our outreach efforts—our job, it seems, is to love and be available.

*****

When I was 15, a local junior high teacher entered my world, and my life has never been the same. Dan Borgman was our Young Life leader, and we casually met the first night I went to the club meeting. The next day, he walked on campus and reintroduced himself using a simple formula—he said my name ("Hi, Chap"), he looked me in the eyes, and he shook my hand. As we talked, just briefly at first, he let me know in his manner and ease that I was safe with him, that he cared about me, and that I mattered to him.

I met Jesus Christ a few months later, after Dan had encouraged me to attend a ski camp. Just a couple of weeks after camp, I moved from Connecticut to California. I missed Dan and the other leaders, but because of them I had been given the gift of knowing Jesus Christ.

In short, they treated me as if they had just read this book.

*****

So what does it mean to "reach out to unchurched teenagers"? What does it look like? How do you plan it, teach it, strategize it? That's what Jonathan McKee has given us in this honest, important book. It is grounded in Scripture, solid in theology, and clear in application. I am grateful for this work not only as a professor in youth, family, and culture, but also as an active youth worker who still weeps for those kids who do not know how deeply God cares for them. Jonathan has not given us another theory on evangelism, but a handbook for decisive, Christ-driven engagement with those we seek to reach.

I know this book will help you because it has helped me, far more than even Jonathan knows. Its roots extend to before he was born, to a mom and a dad who loved him and taught him what it means to love those whom Jesus loves.

I have been changed and affected forever, just like Jonathan, by these people. You see, Jonathan's dad, Tom, was the youth pastor who followed up where Dan Borgman left off with me—a young, brash, enthusiastic new believer, brand-new to California, who needed gentleness, encouragement, and patience in the early years of his spiritual journey.

Of course this book is great—it runs in the genes.

—Chap Clark
Author, *Hurt: Inside the World of Today's Teenagers*
Associate Professor, Youth, Family and Culture, Fuller Theololgical Seminary

chapter 1

Youth Ministry in One Word

Dear Jonathan,

I just graduated from high school, and now I'm working as a youth intern at my church. I've been reading a lot about youth ministry. There are so many different theories as to what is important. Some people say worship. Others say outreach. Others say discipleship. Others say all of those—but make sure you know your purpose.

This is all cool, but the bottom line is that there are a bunch of my friends who have never even come to church. And now that I have graduated and work with teenagers, I see a bunch of the kids at the school in our area who never come to our youth group and activities. What about those kids?

To be completely honest, most churches I've been in are so focused on the kids inside their walls that they've forgotten about the kids outside. And for those of us who do try to do outreach— let's be honest—the outreach ministry of most churches extends only as far as the friends of church kids, and there are a whole lot still left.

I'm thinking we're missing something here. I think we're missing the big picture. I don't want ministry programming tips… just tell me what you think youth ministry is all about. As a matter of fact, just give me the one word you think youth ministry is all about!

Thanks,
Bryan

~

Dear Bryan,

LOVE

Jonathan

~

Dear Jonathan,

Hey, thanks for getting back to me so soon.

Okay, you took me seriously. Now forget all that stuff about one word. Love isn't the answer I want. I mean—it's cool and all—it's probably even right. But I just need you to expand on it a little bit. How do we reach the kids outside our church walls? How do we reach unchurched students?

Bryan

One Word

How do you sum up students reaching other students in one word? How do you verbalize—in one word—youth leaders reaching out to youth?

Let's go to the only place I know to go: the Word of God. Jesus was asked basically the same question in Matthew 22, Mark 12, and Luke 10. The conversation went something like this: "Okay, Jesus—then what is the most important thing? Don't give me the long answer, just what is the bottom line?"

Jesus answered, "Love God…love others."
That's what it comes down to. Love.

Bringing God to People

Our church has a missionary in Laos named Jim Gustufson. Jim told us about a church he visited in Thailand. It was a church founded by Westerners from America, reaching Thai people. Jim told us about a Sunday when he arrived at the church early. Other than himself, the first person to arrive was a woman who walked in dancing, singing in Thai, and praising God for what he had done that week in her life. Two more people walked in singing together and praising God. This happened more and more until the audience was filled with people singing songs in Thai and praising God for what he had done.

Then Jim told us about someone else who walked into the church. This person didn't dance or sing. With his head down, he walked in and stepped onto the stage—and the Lord left! The place went silent as the American pastor took his place on stage, opened the American hymn book as stoically as possible, and announced, "Everyone turn to page 256 and let's begin worship this morning." Ironically, that call to worship ended any worship that was going on.

Many of us use the terminology "bring someone to Christ" or "lead someone to Christ." However, Jim made an important point. In the Bible, the Gospel of John says that when Jesus came to earth, "the Word became flesh and dwelt among us." Jesus left his seat next to God to be with us—to come to us. Let's not forget about the greatest act of love in history—God brought Jesus to us! This American pastor simply brought Western rituals and religion to an Eastern culture. He didn't let the people meet Jesus where they were. Instead he tried to bring them to Jesus via a Western tradition they didn't understand.

We don't need to bring people to Christ; we need to bring Christ to them.

A fast-food restaurant by my house just went out of business. Every time I went in there, the people behind the counter were always rude and preoccupied with their own business. Many times, as I was trying to order my combo number three with no pickles, the cashier would start arguing with the fry guy. Often customers would be waiting for service while the manager was trying to resolve the most recent scheduling problems or employee strife. Well, it wasn't long before they were out of business.

I know why.

They forgot what they were there to do.

They forgot that a fast-food chain does not exist in order to highlight the concerns of those who are working behind the counter. The whole reason a fast-food chain exists is to provide food for the people out there—on the other side of the counter.

Sadly, that can be true of us today. As believers we get so caught up with what's going on inside the church walls while we're shepherding our own people that we forget about the people out there. We forget one of the main reasons we still exist on this planet is to "go and make disciples of all nations."

So how do we reach those who aren't coming into the walls of the church? How do we bring Christ to them? It starts with compassion.

chapter 2

I Thought I Already Had Compassion

Looking at "the unchurched" through different eyes

Amber never realized the effect she had on another's life. For her it was just a typical Tuesday evening youth group. Amber was an eighth grader in this small town and had gone to the same church all of her life. She was pretty accustomed to the Tuesday-night youth group routine by now. She would wait out front for her friend Lindsey to show up in a minivan full of friends. They would all burst out of the car and greet each other with the normal squeaks, squeals, and ritualistic half hugs. Then the small circle would form in order to get caught up on the latest gossip of who's dating whom, who broke up with whom, who hates whom, and so on. Slowly the group would instinctively drift across the church grounds toward the youth group room.

The routine was halted abruptly this week when Amber noticed a small orange light glowing from the shadows against the wall. The group instantly grew silent as they stared at the boy leaning against the wall and smoking a cigarette. He wore baggy pants, a belt that was obviously too big for him, a black shirt, and sunglasses. He had several piercings in various locations on his body and a haircut to match. The awkward pause hung there like a thick fog. Amber broke the silence by scurrying for the door and slipping inside, with her friends just half a step behind. Minutes later they were back to their routine—circled up and giggling at some boys across the room—while the individual who had just entered their lives was forgotten.

The youth leader started playing his guitar and called them all together by saying, "You all know this one." They gathered close to the stage area and started singing. It was then that Amber saw him again. From the corner of her eye she saw him walk into the back of the room and sit against the back wall. *Why was he here? Why is he staying in the back of the room? Does he think he's too good for us?*

After several songs Amber glanced over again. The boy wasn't singing. He was just sitting there with an unchanging expression. The singing, clapping, and hand motions continued, and Amber participated outwardly while she kept an eye on the lone figure in the back of the room. *Why wasn't he singing? Does he think he's too cool?*

The youth leader finished the familiar songs and announced that Lindsey would be giving her testimony. Cheers and whistles brought Lindsey up. Blushing and rocking back and forth from her left to right foot, Lindsey began her canned presentation: "I grew up in a Christian home with two loving parents. I've always tried to be a good Christian, although sometimes it's been tough. I accepted Jesus in my heart when I was five years old in VBS. I've always tried to persevere and keep my eyes on him..."

Amber noticed the boy was staring at Lindsey with a callous expression. *Was he giving her dirty looks? Who does he think he is coming in here, smelling like smoke, thinking he's too good for all of us?*

Lindsey finished, and then the youth pastor gave his talk. Near the end, the boy slipped out the side door, and Amber didn't see him again for two weeks. It was a Sunday morning, and Amber was eating a muffin at the kitchen table when she heard her mom gasp, "Did you know this boy?" Amber's mom turned the newspaper around and slid it across the table. Amber saw a picture of the face she had almost forgotten underneath the headline: *Billy Coleman Takes Own Life with Dad's 38.*

Amber didn't say anything. She just put the muffin down, grabbed the newspaper, and ran into her bedroom. As Amber read the article, she began to feel nauseous. So many emotions overwhelmed her. She was angry when she read about the tough life a young boy had endured. Guilt struck her at the same time, which was quickly thwarted by confusion and excuses—*I didn't know.* That was the bottom line. She didn't know. She didn't know what it was like to be Billy.

Billy

The only reason Billy had shown up at the church was because of a promise to his dying grandfather—the only caring person in Billy's life. Billy never knew his mom. She was a drug addict, so "the system" awarded custody to Billy's alcoholic father and whatever girlfriend he had that particular week.

Billy had only heard the words *I love you* once—from his grandpa—when he was 10 years old. Throughout all his years, the one family member he could tolerate was his grandfather. They wouldn't talk much, but they would fish, and Billy loved it.

Fishing with his grandfather seemed like a dream compared to the reality of Billy's homelife—scurrying by the TV, hoping not to draw too much attention from his father's form lying in the recliner.

Billy started running around with an older group of kids that cruised around the neighborhoods at night. They all smoked and Billy quickly learned to fit in.

Billy only went to church two times. Once when his baby cousin got water sprinkled on him in that big white church downtown, and once when his grandpa died. This was just a couple weeks before Billy took his own life. Billy's weekly fishing trips with his grandpa slipped to every other month or so as Billy became more involved with his friends. One day when Billy got home, his dad wasn't there. The current girlfriend told Billy that his dad was at the hospital visiting Billy's grrandpa. He was dying.

When Billy got to the hospital, his dad had already left. His grandpa was awake and had tubes and wires hooked all over his body. When his grandpa saw him, his eyes lit up. Billy went to his side and sat down. Billy looked at his grandfather as if to ask if everything was all right. His grandfather looked back, his expression saying no. Billy sunk lower in his chair, and they sat in silence, wishing they were on the old 16-foot boat.

Finally, his grandfather broke the silence. "Billy, I want you to do something for me."

"What?"

"I want you to go to my church."

Billy felt his own body getting tight, his shoulders rising. His face muscles clenched and tears started to form in the corners of his eyes. "All right, Grandpa."

Billy sat there for another hour and a half. They didn't say another word. They just sat there together comfortably, sharing their last moment the way they always had, as Billy's grandpa slowly slipped away.

Billy noticed a poster in the back of the church on the way out of his grandfather's funeral. The poster said something about a junior high group on Tuesday nights. Billy scanned the necessary information and left the building.

Tuesday night came and Billy set out to keep his promise. When he got to the church he went to what the map on the poster described as the "youth room." He saw a couple of kids inside and was a little early, so he did what he always did—propped up against an inconspicuous wall and lit up a cigarette.

Five girls approached, laughing and giggling, at least until one of them caught sight of Billy. Billy kept his eyes on the girls, reading every one of their faces as they stood there in silence. Finally one girl led them to safety inside the room, leaving Billy to finish his cigarette. Billy finished his cigarette and decided he had better keep his promise. He hoped there wasn't something he was supposed to do in this place. *Do I need a school ID? What if I'm not supposed to be here? Are they going to ask me if I'm their religion?* When he walked in, suspicious eyes examined him, wondering why he was there, why he wasn't with anyone, and who had invited him.

Billy was rejected—again. Everyone kept looking at him. They used words he didn't understand. They constantly used the word *Christian,* which confused Billy because his dad always told him they were Christians by birth. Billy remembered walking by the Santa ringing a bell in front of the stores every Christmas season. His dad would always slip a dollar in the little red pot and tell Billy, "It's the Christian thing to do."

Billy finally had enough. He left the youth room just before the meeting was over, wondering what his grandpa wanted him to find in that place. He missed his grandpa. He wished they could go fishing just one more time. He longed to see his grandpa's gaze and slow, steady smile.

Two weeks later, late on a Friday night, Billy felt emptier than he had ever felt before as he came home from a party absolutely wasted. Sometimes drinking made his problems go away, but they always came back. He didn't see an end in sight, and an end meant "peace." So he created one with his father's revolver.

Amber never knew what it was like to be Billy. It never entered her mind. Amber, like many of us, lived in her own world and only saw her surroundings through her own eyes—until one day her eyes were opened. Amber put herself in Billy's shoes and felt Billy's pain. She felt it so strongly that she got sick to her stomach. For the first time in her life, she was looking at someone who was different from her, and she felt *compassion.*

There are plenty of Billys out there. Not all of them have been dealt such a bad hand, but because they seem so different from us we don't understand them. Reaching out to them begins with *compassion.*

How I Got Compassion

During all four of my high school years I worked as a student leader in my youth group. I also worked with teenagers off and on during college, running big church programs and helping on various youth staffs. I knew how to lead games, how to make youth laugh, how to make hilarious videos. I knew how to talk to teenagers and relate to them. I liked students and hung around them. But something was missing.

As I look back to my years and years of "doing the youth leader thing," even though on the outside it may have looked like I was doing all the right things, I never looked beyond the walls of the youth group room. And if you had asked me why I was there, I probably would have told you, "for the kids." But I really didn't know what that meant. I guess the best way to describe my role was "chaperone." I just wandered in, made sure things ran smoothly, and wandered out.

Sure, there were those times we worked on the lesson for the day. All of us simply put on our Bible-mode faces, trudged through the small group questions, and thought about where we were going to eat when we were done with all of this. It's embarrassing to admit I thought that way, but I just wasn't aware of the need out there. I wasn't aware of the majority of the population that wasn't making it to our little youth group or to our church on Sunday. I needed my eyes opened.

In 1993, God opened my eyes. In September of that year, I started a campus outreach to a needy group of students on a junior high campus. At the time, the school administration didn't let us meet on campus, so we invited the kids over to our house. What started with seven students grew to 12, then 23, then 26, and finally about 35 to 40 students weekly. We eventually moved to my garage, where we put eight old couches around the edges with a section of carpet in the middle.

I can still remember the first night when my wife, Lori, my infant son Alec, and I sat down with seven of those students over a pizza. One by one they shared their lives. Later that night Lori and I lay awake in tears most of the night. These students broke our hearts.

The following is an old prayer letter I found that sums up my thoughts at that time of my life:

March 1994

Dear Friends,

I really struggled writing this letter this month. I am seeing so much pain and hopelessness around me that I am growing weary. I never thought I would be shocked by the violence, hatred, and bitter attitudes that pour from our youth; and in reality, I'm not shocked by the youth—I'm shocked by the adults who let it happen...

...One of the girls in our group has been tugging on all our hearts the last few weeks. She shows up to our Thursday-night outreach sometimes an hour early and never wants to go back home. We realized Cindy isn't very well-off when she showed up to our snow event in the same pair of shorts she had worn the last week. She said her "pair of pants" was being washed. Her home situation is very poor. Her 16-year-old sister had a baby and left it with her parents to raise while she lives with her boyfriend (who doesn't like kids). Cindy's 19-year-old sister has just had her second child from her boyfriend, and they live in the living room of her parents' house. The only person in that house with a job is Cindy's dad, who's actually on disability again. Her mom encourages the sisters to hold on to the boyfriends they have now, in fear that they might not find others. She ignores the fact that this live-in boyfriend hits Cindy's sister, as well as Cindy, whenever they get in the way. Nevertheless, my wife, Lori, has had some neat talks with her, and Cindy really likes her. She responded well to the idea of spending some time with Lori throughout the week. Please keep Cindy in prayer.

I lay awake half the night, restless after spending time with these kids who are growing up way too fast. Pray that we can provide the role models they lack. Pray that in their emptiness, they can feel how Christ can fill them. Pray that they can see his love through us. We are fatigued, but we see progress. I am glad my staff and my family have the opportunity to make a difference.

Sincerely,
Jonathan

Ministry starts with a broken heart. Reaching out to the unchurched around us starts with *compassion.*

Jesus and Compassion

Jesus traveled, preached, and healed during his public ministry. There was no one like him—and his amazing power to heal and reach into people's hearts gained him an incredibly large following.

Have you ever considered Jesus' incredible following? Have you considered how many people would mob someone who has the power to heal? Think about it.

I have really bad eyesight. I've had a cornea transplant in each eye, and I constantly have problems with them. And now there's a list of sports I can't play and activities I'm not supposed to do because of my weak corneas. (Some I do anyway, much to my wife's disapproval.) If I lived in Palestine 2,000 years ago, you can bet I would have been in the front lines of those crowds, or in a tree with Zacchaeus, or hitching a ride on that mat descending from the ceiling so I could get my eyes fixed! Jesus was flat out *healing* people.

Naturally when Jesus would try to go and be alone, the crowds of people would find him anyway and gather. Once he even got in a boat to go across a lake. The crowds ran around the lake and gathered on the other side.

So Jesus often found himself tired, hungry…and watching people gather. He saw tax collectors and probably got evil stares from everyone as they approached him. He saw prostitutes and adulterous women. He saw families fighting, people shoving and trying to get in front of each other. He saw Pharisees looking down on everyone and plotting evil things against him.

As Jesus sat and watched all of this, I would expect him to do what I'd be tempted to do—get even with those scummy people. I think he'd want to rub his hands together, form a big lightning bolt, zap the entire crowd, and send them straight to hell. But he didn't. He had compassion for them.

This happens in Matthew 9. The word used in the Bible to describe the way Jesus felt means "a pain deep in one's bowels." Jesus felt such compassion for the lost that he literally got pains in his stomach.

How do you feel when you see non-Christians in this world? Many of us might identify with gut pains when we hear about starving children or when we see helpless elderly people with no one to care for them. But what do we feel when we see the unchurched—especially if they're hard to love? What about that student who drives us crazy?

She Drives Me Crazy

Years ago we had a student named Jenny who drove everyone nuts. The kids used to make fun of her and were downright mean to her. Once when she walked into a room full of junior high students, a student turned to another and said, "Now that's the face of the devil himself!" We felt sorry for Jenny, but she didn't just drive students her own age nuts—she drove us all nuts! There were times she arrived, and I saw all of my staff slowly hide behind other students, hoping to avoid her.

One day, Kristi, a new volunteer, decided to start helping our small junior high outreach. Kristi let me know right away that she didn't know how to lead any games or activities, she didn't know how to talk to kids, and she didn't know if she could answer many questions about the Bible. She also made me promise her that I would never make her talk in front of the group. The first week she came, Jenny ran up to Kristi and introduced herself. My staff all cringed, preparing their good-byes to Kristi, knowing she would probably never come back. But that night at the staff meeting something amazing happened. Each staff member was sharing which students they were getting to know better and with whom they wanted to spend more time. Kristi shared that she had talked with Jenny and wondered if she could start spending some time with her. All my staff responded immediately, "Yes!", "Absolutely!", and "Please do!" None of us said a word, of course, and we trod through the rest of the meeting cautiously, wondering if we really were going to get away with passing Jenny off on poor Kristi.

Over the next year Kristi—who couldn't lead games, didn't know how to talk to kids, couldn't answer questions about the Bible, and couldn't speak in front of a crowd—loved Jenny for who she was. As the year passed, Jenny changed. My staff and I couldn't believe it. Kristi had a broken heart for Jenny. We all saw a loud, annoying, rude junior high kid; but Kristi saw an empty kid who needed love and attention desperately.

I'll never forget the night when Kristi came up to me with Jenny. They both had tears in their eyes and smiles from ear to ear. Kristi told me that Jenny wanted to tell me something. Jenny announced, "I gave my life to Jesus!" and then she burst into tears. We all hugged her and shed tears of our own.

What Are We Going To Do?

Reaching the unchurched starts with compassion. God gives us compassion when we stop thinking of ourselves, and we ask two vital questions:

1. What is it like to be _____?

2. What would Jesus want me to do?

What is it like to be Billy? What is it like to be Jenny? What is it like to be our neighbor who we see at the mailbox every day? What is it like to be that person at the copy machine at work? This question gets rid of self and considers others. It also raises the other question: What would Jesus want me to do?

We all remember the big "What Would Jesus Do?" campaign. I've spoken at many camps, retreats, and Christian leadership events where "WWJD?" bracelets were handed out to kids who wanted to ask that question. This was a great campaign, but I am challenging you to ask a different question.

We all have different strengths. Billy Graham had a much different ministry that Mother Teresa. Should Billy Graham have stopped preaching, rolled up his sleeves, and started nursing the sick? Should Mother Teresa have abandoned her ministry and started preaching nationally? No. Jesus has something different and incredible planned for each of us. When our hearts are broken, and we put ourselves in someone else's shoes, then the question to ask ourselves is, "What would Jesus want *me* to do?"

Sharing our faith starts with compassion. Compassion asks: What's it like to be [fill in the blank], and what does Jesus want *me* to do about it?

But to really know what it's like to be Billy or Jenny or any unchurched teenager, we need to get into their heads.

chapter 3

In the Minds of Unchurched Students

Why they think
what they think

I was on campus one day talking with some church kids about our upcoming weekend retreat. They were introducing me to some of the friends they'd invited to go with us on the trip. I looked across the cafeteria at a group of boys wearing basketball jerseys. I asked the church kids, "How about those guys? Has anyone invited them?"

The church kids whispered, "You wouldn't want any of them—they're atheists."

"Atheists?"

"Yeah. They party all the time and—just trust me. You don't want them!"

Was it true? Was the entire basketball team comprised of atheists? I went over and talked with these students and invited them to our weekly event. In the months following, I got to know several of these "atheists." Some were definitely on the wild side, but several of them went to church occasionally. Most of them were comfortable talking about God. None of them were atheists.

Why do Christians sometimes assume that just because someone doesn't go to church, he must be an atheist? The fact is, many of us don't understand unchurched kids. And this misunderstanding often keeps us from reaching them.

To reach unchurched kids we first need to understand them.

Five Facts About Unchurched Kids

1. Unchurched kids believe that any belief or religion is okay, as long as it helps YOU!

Seeing people's reactions when they find out that I'm a minister is always entertaining. I was getting my hair cut a few months ago and my occupation came up in the conversation. The stylist paused at first, but then she said, "Oh, that's nice." Then there was the second pause—which I refer to as the "What am I going to say next to cover up the awkward silence?" pause—followed by, "You know, people need that." So she started sharing how Native Americans, Buddhists, Christians (her religion of claim), and Hindus all have truths we can learn from. "They all pretty much teach the same thing."

Today there is a growing trend toward universalism. All paths lead to God—or eternal peace or heaven—in one form or another. Most students don't believe Jesus Christ is the only way to heaven. Our culture values diversity but ignores any contradictions. So more and more people are allowing that all religious faiths have value and offer equally effective solutions. In America's spirit of tolerance, people often value all religions and belief systems—even if they contradict one another.

This generation of students is "tolerant" of all beliefs and, consequently, can't understand why all paths *don't* lead to God. "If I share Jesus with one of my friends, she might think Jesus sounds cool." Realistically, they will probably think he is *a way* to happiness and inner peace, just not *the way*.

Unchurched youth don't believe that only one way of thinking is correct. "How do we really know what is true? What is true for you might not be true for me because we're all different. There is no such thing as right or wrong, so every answer could be right." This belief is common. Some call it pluralism. Pluralism embraces and tolerates multiple viewpoints, often concluding that there is no wrong answer; therefore, anything can be right. Others call it postmodernism, which doesn't value absolute truth. Both of these overlap quite a bit. I'm not going to get into a debate in semantics, but I do want to recognize this mind-set that we'll come across.

This perspective of "everything can be right" or "nothing is certain" bleeds into any conversation we have about morality. We'll witness this when we talk with unchurched students about decision making, whether they are small decisions like cheating or lying, or major life decisions like sleeping with someone or having an abortion. Although *we* may see these choices as having clear-cut right or wrong answers, they may not think it's so clear. They might ask us, "How can you say something is 'just wrong' like that? That may be true for you, but how can you say it's true for me or anyone else? For me it might be okay."

As our society dumps many biblical beliefs or any absolute truth, for that matter, more students are willing to accept any religion or belief as a viable solution in a given situation. They are growing to believe that any religion or belief is probably okay as long as it works for you.

Teenage role models express similar opinions. In the May 23, 2002, issue of *Rolling Stone* magazine, *Spiderman's* Kirsten Dunst was quoted as saying: "I think a lot of people are losing their religion. Definitely. Even me, I know that when I grew up, I used to go to church every Sunday, and now it's become holidays. But I think as long as you have your own thing, whether it's meditation—anything that centers you in life is good. Do I pray? Yeah, I do" (p. 69).

That summarizes today's mind-set well—"As long as you have something that centers your life, it's okay."

2. Unchurched kids are intrigued by the spiritual...and repelled by religion.

Today's teenagers are very interested in spiritual things, but they still don't want something running their lives!

Some of us may be surprised by the first part of that statement. Many Christians incorrectly assume that because the "unchurched" aren't at church they must not be interested in God. But the majority of the unchurched are very interested in God or the afterlife. They just don't want to give up control of their lives to God or some religion.

George Barna, in his August 26, 2002, *Barna Update*, notes that we are "a nation where most people call themselves 'deeply spiritual' and where four out of five adults say their religious faith is very important in their life."

91 percent of American women pray.

85 percent of American men pray.

1 in 5 atheists pray.

Yet, in total, 83 percent of teenagers maintain that moral truth depends on the circumstances, and only 6 percent believe that moral truth is absolute (Barna, 2001).

People today are highly spiritual, but they shy away from any kind of formal religion. They believe in an eternal spirit and life after death but don't want to read the Bible, attend church, or change their lifestyles.

Teenage role models are very clear on this issue as well:

"My grandma's very religious, and I went to Catholic school. But I'm kind of an ex-Catholic now. I'm a spiritual person, but I have minimal religion" (Actor Josh Hartnett responding to a question about religion in *YM* magazine, June 2002, p. 111).

"I still see hip-hop as a religion but as a Buddhist sort of thing, not an extremist, fundamentalist thing. It's a lens that I view everything through: culturally, politically, ideologically..." (Josh Davis—a.k.a., "DJ Shadow" the hip-hop monk quoted in *SPIN*, July 2002, p. 97).

"I like spirituality, not religion or politics. Religion turns into 'My god's bigger than your god; therefore, you're a heathen, and you should die, and I'll take your land and build a temple on top of your flattened house.' Religion is a corrupt business... Spirituality is like water and sun. When it rains, the prostitute and the pope get wet just the same. Spirituality is not memorizing the Koran or the Bible while hurting people in the name of Allah or Jesus or Buddha or oil. We are all chosen. Surely we have the capacity to transmute anger and fear into a masterpiece of joy" (Carlos Santana, *USA Today*, October 16, 2002).

"I worship God. Religion and worship are two different things to me. Religion is by the book. I think too many people rely on the textbook: okay, it says to do this and it says to do that, so if I do this, this, and that, then I still can go out and do wrong because I did this, this, and that. God is my best friend. I talk to God every day. And no one can tell me how to talk to God, not no imam, not no priest, not no rabbi, no pastor" (Hip-hop artist Eve quoted from the September/October 2002 issue of *Complex* magazine, p. 94).

The message is clear. Today's teenagers don't want something running their lives. "All this religious talk is cool, but don't tell me to stop sleeping with my girlfriend, to stop smoking pot, or to start forgiving my dad!"

3. Unchurched kids don't know what Christianity is.

When my son Alec was six, he came home from first grade and announced how happy he was that his new friend was a "Christian." I asked him how he knew. He said, "I asked her, and she said that her dad said she was."

Well then, it's settled. If her dad says she is—she must be!

Sometimes we assume that when people say the word *Christian*, they mean a person who has accepted Jesus as their Lord and Savior. We often assume people know the differences between denominations and can distinguish a cult member from our biblical definition of a Christian. When you say the word *Christian*, people might think you are the guys on the mountain bikes that go door to door. Or you might be the ones who can't celebrate holidays. Or maybe you go to church on Saturday because that's what you're supposed to do. People don't know what's what, and they lump it all together.

Eighty-two percent of teenagers claimed they were "Christian" in 1999. Two out of three (67 percent) unchurched adults call themselves Christian (Barna, 2000). Wow! That sounds pretty good, huh? Then how come 46 percent of the "unchurched" don't even know why we celebrate Easter? And only 13 percent of Americans still believe in the Ten Commandments? And just seven percent of teenagers say their moral choices were based on biblical principles? We've got a bunch of people calling themselves "Christian" who don't believe in the Bible or really put their faith in Christ and all he stands for.

When we hear people call themselves Christians, we assume they've examined the Christian faith. We assume they've given their life to Jesus, the only way to God. But people are actually using the word very differently. Most of the "unchurched" today view Christianity as a heritage, not a relationship with God.

I was with an "unchurched" student at his house when the word *Christian* came up in our conversation. He quickly responded, "Oh, I'm a Christian."

I said, "Cool, when did you become a Christian?"

He looked confused and then hollered to his grandma in the other room, "Grandma, am I a Christian?"

She hollered back, "No, you're a Presbyterian!"

Many unchurched students don't know what they are. As far as they know, they are whatever Mom says.

And sometimes people can sound like very sincere Christians. Justin Timberlake was quoted as saying, "I can honestly say I am a Christian, but my spirituality has been developed on the road and is based on my experiences with God" (*Rolling Stone*, January 23, 2003, p. 38).

This sounds convincing. But read another quote from Justin: "I believe in the spiritual afterlife. I believe, in some shape or form, in past-life regression and souls coming back to Earth for unfinished business. You know, when you run into people and you're like, 'I know I've met you somewhere'? I think maybe you actually did. I think that's what soul mates means—that you were connected to that person in a past life" (*Blender* magazine, December 2002, p. 60).

Talking with kids today, we might hear a lot of them claiming Christianity. But this country is the same place where three out of five teenagers (61 percent) agree that "if a person is generally good or does enough good things for others during their life, they will earn a place in heaven" (Barna, 2000). And 64 percent of unchurched adults state that a good person can earn his or her way into heaven (Barna, 2000).

Let's face it. The unchurched don't know what Christianity really is.

4. Unchurched kids don't know what they believe.

Britney Spears tells the German magazine *Cinema* that she has a pretty clear idea of who God is. In the great beyond, "everyone is at peace and happy, and they all hop around from cloud to cloud. In heaven you can see your grandparents and everyone you loved once again. And an old man with a long white beard wanders around, that's God."

Today's youth have all kinds of theories about God and about life after death. I'll never forget a conversation I had with a high school senior named James. He always argued against Jesus being the only way. He was drilling me and questioning my beliefs when I asked him, "James, what do you believe?"

He stopped for a moment and thought. Then he started to fumble out his beliefs. "I think that there is a something out there—like a vapor or something—that is in charge of everything. This vapor is powerful, but lets us do our own thing. It doesn't care if we party or anything like that—but it can help us if we want. But it also...I guess it also sees who is good, but...you know..." then he stopped, totally confused and said, "Does this sound stupid?"

Some students come up with empty philosophies to "fill the gap." They come up with reasoning or logic for their actions because inside they're searching for answers; and if they can't find them, they try to provide their own. So often these self-made answers are simply a way to justify what feels good.

Singer and actress Brandy (Norwood) gives her theory on this: "I know my purpose. I couldn't say that before. Three years ago I couldn't say that I knew why I was here. My purpose is to experience love and just be who I am, and whatever that is, that's all I have to do. I don't have to do anything else but be myself" (AP, April 3, 2002).

Jennifer Lopez has a similar theory: "I only do what my gut tells me to... if it doesn't feel right to me, there's just no way that I'm going to do it. You're the only one that can tell you what's right for you" (_Cosmo Girl_, June/July 2002, pp. 36, 39).

Barna concludes from his research that, "By far the most common basis for moral decision-making was doing whatever feels right or comfortable in a situation."

Fifty-one percent of Americans have no life philosophy. The unchurched we work with might seem sure they don't want Jesus, but the truth is that they really don't know what they want. They just want something to fill the emptiness.

5. Unchurched kids are looking for something to fill the emptiness.

Years ago Madonna said the following in a *Vogue* interview: "I have an iron will, and all of my will has always been devoted to conquering some horrible feelings of inadequacy. I'm always struggling with that fear. I push past one spell of it and discover myself as a special human being of worth, and then I get to another stage and I think I'm mediocre and uninteresting and worthless, and I have to find a way to get myself out of that again and again. My drive in life is from this horrible feeling of being inadequate and mediocre and it is always pushing me, and pushing me and pushing me. Because even though I have become somebody, I still have to prove that I am SOMEBODY. My struggle has never ended and it probably never will."

The "unchurched" student is looking for something to fill the hole in her heart. But she's trying to fill that void with things that were never designed to fit there—possessions, popularity, drugs, alcohol, etc. But nothing works. So she continues to question.

Wallis Burks, 16, a sophomore at Sacred Heart Academy, said the following in an interview: "If I stated right now that I am an atheist and I don't believe in a God—in your mind you're probably like 'devil worshiper'… I seriously don't believe in a God or a devil or heaven or hell at this point in my life. I'm like a questioner. That's what I do. I sit in class all day, and I ask questions." ("A Question of Faith," *The Courier-Journal*, March 16).

The unchurched just want purpose. Rick Warren's *The Purpose Driven Life* sold like hotcakes for that very reason.

We've got what unchurched kids want, the only thing that will fill their emptiness—a relationship with Jesus Christ.

Christine's Search

I'll never forget a girl named Christine who made a point of telling me that she was an atheist. She was one of the many unchurched kids who came to our campus outreach; and the first week she attended, she stood up in the middle of my talk and headed for the door.

My wife, Lori, went out and asked her what was wrong. Christine quickly retorted, "If I knew you were going to talk about God, I wouldn't have come! I'm an atheist."

Lori calmed her down and somehow convinced her to hang out a few more minutes. I finally got a chance to talk with her. She quickly told me the same thing she had told Lori. "I'm an atheist. I don't want to talk about all this God stuff!"

I told her, "I'm willing to respect that." But then I asked her a question, "Can you respect the fact that I believe in God?"

I think that caught her off guard. But Christine was smart, and she realized that it seemed only fair. "Sure, I can respect that."

"Great." I replied. "Around here—we really want to hear from you. This is a safe place to talk about your life, your dreams, your fears, your struggles, and your beliefs. I'm happy to listen to what you have to say, and sometimes you can listen to what we have to say."

She thought about it for a moment, then stuck out her hand. "Deal."

So we agreed. I'd be tolerant of her disbelief, and she'd be tolerant of our belief. And she would respect us when we shared our beliefs, and we would respect her if she shared her disbelief in her small group or in times of interaction.

Christine came to our ministry for months. She was a delightful girl, and everyone enjoyed her. But whenever the subject of God came up, she always made it clear she didn't believe in him in any way, often verbalizing it to everyone. During Easter discussions she only wanted to talk about bunnies and eggs. During Christmas discussions it was only Santa and reindeer for Christine.

Finally, one day we all went to a local Christian concert event. Christine liked bands, and she was excited to hear the music. But she also knew that a speaker was scheduled at the event. She made a point of asking me, "Is that speaker going to talk about God?"

I was honest with her, "Oh, I'm sure he is. He's been through a lot. And God helped him through it, so I'm sure he'll mention that."

"Well, I don't want to hear about that."

"You know what you believe," I offered, "and he knows what he believes. Why don't you just check out what he's got to say. He tells some great stories!"

She thought about it again, silently nodded, and went back to her friends.

The band played, and the speaker got up and told his story. He shared how he had pushed God away his entire life until he finally realized that God was just what he needed. Then he invited the crowd to give their lives to Jesus. I knew this was my cue to help with counseling. I remember looking around and hoping some of the kids I brought would come forward. I actually remember thinking, *Okay, Christine can stay and watch our stuff while I go down to talk with some of the people who come forward.*

But when I looked for Christine—she was gone.

I looked down the aisle and there she was, heading for the stage.

I ran down the aisle, and asked her, "Christine, what are you doing?" I figured she had gone up there to hassle the speaker or to try to convince people to turn back.

She wiped the tears from her eyes. "I'm coming forward."

I said. "I can see that. But why?" I wasn't getting it.

"I want to give my life to God."

After several people revived me, holding smelling salts to my nose, I asked her, "Why do you want to do that?"

She said, "I've spent my whole life pushing him away. I figure it's time to stop fighting it."

The Secret Need

No matter how much unchurched students seem to want to push God away, secretly they are looking for something to fill the emptiness in their lives. Lee Strobel, author of the book _The Case for Christ_, attested to this in his earlier book, _Inside the Mind of Unchurched Harry & Mary_.

I asked Lee, an ex-atheist, about this in an interview I had with him for our ministry's e-zine newsletter:

JONATHAN: In that book (_Harry & Mary_), one of your points was that "people are morally adrift but secretly want an anchor." An encouraging point to those of us sharing our faith—because of the ramifications—"people want something more than the empty life they're leading—whether they admit it or not!" Yesterday you shared that, as an atheist, you felt like something was missing. But because you didn't want to feel guilty about your behavior, you used to use your atheism as an excuse for your actions...?

LEE: Well, I think that atheists...in my experience, have some intellectual, and sometimes considerably intellectual issues involved with Christianity. But often those are used to mask underlying moral or emotional issues that, I think, were both true in my case. I think the questions I had intellectually were legitimate, but at the same time I used them, not as a platform to pursue truth, but a defense mechanism to keep Christianity away. So it didn't infringe upon my morals or cause me to deal with emotional issues that kept me away from God.

JONATHAN: So when you wrote that point about "secretly wanting an anchor," was that strictly from your life or did you observe people having this up-front shell but underneath feeling empty?

LEE: Well, my friends in the newspaper business who lived very raucous, wild lives, as people I think really deep down inside, they were coming to the realization that this is not the path to happiness. That it was not leading them where they wanted to go. And yet they knew nothing else but to continue to pursue it. And I think down inside they were looking for some framework for their lives—some anchor for their lives. And, some have found it and many of them haven't.

Mind Matters

Sometimes it's hard to relate to unchurched students. But if you get a peek at what might be going on inside their heads, you can understand them and have compassion toward them. And there's a lot going on in the minds of unchurched students. But before we can show them the answer, we need to make sure we have it ourselves.

chapter 4

A Rude Awakening

How I finally realized that "sharing my faith" starts with MY faith

The Sunday school teacher moved the little paper apostle Paul across the flannel graph board to talk to the little paper prison guard. In a very low, apostle-Paul-like voice, the teacher would exclaim, "The reason I didn't break out of prison is because God loves you and has a wonderful plan for your life!" Then turning to us, she would always say, "And we need to be sure to share our faith with our friends and neighbors and schoolmates."

Share our faith. Share our faith? Isn't that one of those phrases that Christians have thrown around for so long in the church that we never actually think about what it means? Is it as common as the words to "A Mighty Fortress is Our God" or as familiar as the contour of the pew? Growing up the son of a Baptist minister, I heard that phrase all the time. I heard it from the missionaries who would come to eat lunch with us after they spoke in the church service. I heard it at the little pep rally we had each year before we would go out and knock on inner-city doors to talk to people about a relationship with God. But somehow I didn't really understand what the words *share our faith* meant.

For much of my life I associated "sharing my faith" with giving out tracts. The local Christian bookstore has tons of them displayed between the newest pieces of apocalyptic fiction and the fish-shaped key chains. And I'm sure someone could save many souls with the tract, "Chemical War: Are You Prepared?"

Later I associated "sharing my faith" with standing up for Christ in certain situations. Of course, my behavior *outside* of these situations didn't seem as important. All through high school, when I wasn't getting suspended or beaten up, I was sure to "share my faith" by standing up for Christian beliefs in the classroom. I remember being remarkably bold during my 10th-grade biology class one day. The theory of evolution was being taught, and I made it clear to the class that I didn't believe in that because I was a Christian, and the Bible taught something else. But a month later I got suspended from the class for cheating.

Despite the sound principles I had been taught my whole life, I somehow convinced myself that my actions didn't matter. I sold out to the same kind of thinking that much of today's generation subscribes to—I had a religion or set of beliefs, but I didn't totally connect them to my day-to-day actions and attitudes.

"Wherever we go—share the gospel. And if absolutely necessary—use words!" Maybe I could have learned from that phrase during my high school years. Our actions do speak much louder than our words. Yet, as much as I like St. Francis of Assisi's age-old phrase, it paves an easy escape route for many of us. "My actions share the gospel, so *I* don't need to! I'll just leave that to the pastors, evangelists, and missionaries."

Starting with Our Own Changed Lives

So what does "sharing our faith" mean? It's more than just a gospel presentation. It's more than a day spent feeding the poor. It's more than any tract, action, or spoken word. It's a spreading fire that catches from one person to another. It starts with our own changed lives. Once we realize the incredible treasure we have, we can't help but share it with others.

In the early '90s I decided to go into full-time ministry. I loved working with youth, and I could see they needed fulfillment in their lives. If anyone would have asked me what I thought they needed during that time—what the missing piece was in their lives—I would have told them without hesitation: God. Unfortunately, I think I was blind to the fact that there was something missing in my life as well. If you had asked me back then what filled me up and gave me hope and purpose, I would have quickly told you, "God." I had the right answer, just like the rich young ruler who immediately gave the right answer to Jesus. But I wonder what would have happened if Jesus had stood there and asked me for everything: my thoughts, my desires, my passions, my time, my relationships—the whole banana. I just wonder if I would have walked away sad.

But then something weird happened.

In 1993, Youth for Christ in Sacramento had a big junior high event. I was there to help facilitate the program, and that was my gift—I was good at it. One night tons of students came forward to respond to an altar call and give their lives to Christ. There were more youth than expected, so my boss turned to me, handed me a book, and said, "Jonathan, we need you to be a counselor."

I quickly replied, "Sure, no problem," assuming my role as the youth expert that I thought I was. I walked over, and two students were introduced to me. They followed me to a corner of the room where we sat in a small circle of three chairs. I asked them why they came forward, and they both said something to the effect of wanting to give their lives to Jesus. Then I realized something—I had nothing to tell them.

I had received Billy Graham's training back in 1984. I had memorized "Steps to Peace with God", "The Four Spiritual Laws"—in English and in Spanish—and I had studied Christian Doctrine, New Testament and Old Testament at my esteemed Christian college. The small tract in my hand contained the words I had said thousands of times before—but I had nothing to say to these two small boys.

I had told myself, "I don't need this tract! I'll just tell them in my own words." But I just stared at them in silence for a few minutes and soon realized there was nothing burning inside of me that I was really excited about sharing with them. I had strutted up to those boys alone, not wanting anyone else there because I knew what I was doing—or so I thought. As I sat there and stared into their eyes—I was completely alone. Sure, I had a bunch of knowledge, tons of ability, resources, skills, and training—but it was all living inside a smelly corpse of a body that was simply going through the motions, saying what I was supposed to say, and doing what I was supposed to do, convinced I could do it on my own. I'm sure Satan had a party that night when he saw how I botched up the simplest of gospel presentations. I still think about those two little boys today and wonder.

The Realization

The following Monday I went into the office of my supervisor with my tail between my legs. No one knew what had happened, but I did. After that I finally realized the most important thing—I can't do it on my own! Not just leading people to Christ, I'm talking about *life*! I can't do it on my own. I needed help. And once I realized that, I became a sponge. I wanted to know everything about living my life for Christ and reaching others. I went to every training session available. I started taking copious notes in church, at outreaches, and even during meetings with people in whom God was working.

Something amazing started happening. My personal relationship with God started growing. The more I realized what a scumbag I was, the more I realized how much I needed him. It also convinced me how much God must really love me because I was hard to love. (Just ask my wife!)

God is an amazing God. I have turned my back on him so many times. I'm not talking about burning upside-down crucifixes and biting off the heads of chickens. I'm just talking about the normal daily stuff. God says, "Trust me, I know what's best for you." And sometimes we just respond, "You know, God, in most situations that would be cool, but right now I know what I'm doing. So if you'd just back off and let me lose my temper here, then everything will be under control!" Then, of course, we realize five minutes later what fools we were.

And here's the amazing thing. If I were God, I would be standing there with my arms crossed, tapping my foot, saying, "I told you so!" But he's not like that. He's there with his arms open wide, and he loves us just the same. This realization has helped me because now the phrases, "God loves you and has a wonderful plan for your life," or "God loves you and wants a personal relationship with you," or "God loves you and wants to be your friend" have more meaning. They aren't just the first lines in a gospel tract; they are a reality—the reality that he is there every day when I mess up, loving me no matter what, filling me when I'm feeling empty, and comforting me when I'm feeling alone.

My life is just one big gospel presentation made real. Every day I see how much God loves me and craves a relationship with me. Every day I see how much I don't deserve his love and his grace because of my failure and lack of trust. Every day I cling to Jesus and the ultimate sacrifice he made so I can have a relationship with him. Every day I trust in him by putting aside my own ways and trusting the ways he has for me. This trust is what started my lifelong relationship with him.

I'm not perfect; I'm still under construction. If we walk around like our lives are all perfect now that we have Jesus, we're not only liars, but our false fronts are also going to make others think we're full of it. Our imperfect, under construction, growing, changing lives are living testimonies of God's grace, power, and our need for him.

Sharing our faith starts with *our faith*. If our faith is weak, then we'll have nothing to share. If our faith is strong and growing, then we'll begin to see through different eyes. We won't be as worried about or influenced by temporary things. Our thoughts and actions will have an eternal focus that gives us the strength to press on in daily life. These eyes also see the people around us searching for something to fill their emptiness and trying to fill it with temporary things that cause pain and suffering. We have the answer, and the world needs it desperately.

chapter 5

Do They *Run* When They See You Coming?

How to *NEVER* reach students

Do they smile or groan when they see you coming? Or do you even know? To truly understand unchurched kids we need to be aware of their perceptions of us. Unfortunately, our reputation isn't good.

Jacob Aranza, a youth speaker who works with unchurched kids, says, "The problem in our day isn't that people don't believe in Jesus; the problem is that people don't believe in *people* who believe in Jesus." People think we're hypocrites, and, let's face it—we are!

I saw a bumper sticker that read "God, please protect me from your followers." This sticker sheds a lot of light on the perception that the unchurched have of Christians and the church.

Singer Boy George said:

On Sunday I attended the christening of my year-old godson Michael, and he was as restless as everyone else. The priest was a lovely man with impeccable dress sense, but I was confused from the moment he took the pulpit. Most of us only ever go to church for weddings and funerals, so sticking to the Book is pointless...

and what's the point of rattling on about sin when most of us are doomed to eternal damnation? It doesn't warm people to Christianity, it only makes them feel like hypocrites. Worse still are the utterly depressing hymns. I'd like to see live music, acoustic guitars, and percussion. Church should be a joyous and liberating experience—[it] badly needs a face-lift because it is God's theatre on earth, and he should be packing them in (*London's Daily Mail*, February 23, 2000).

I spent years of my ministry inviting unchurched youth to church. I almost always got the same responses:

"I don't do church."

"No way, they just want my money."

"I don't need someone else telling me how to live my life!"

Do the unchurched really know who we are? The "Christian" title is slapped on a great number of people in this world: TV evangelists begging for money and bopping people on the head to heal them from their afflictions, abortion clinic bombers, white supremacists wearing crosses or a swastikas, and gay bashers with hate-filled eyes yelling memorized passages of condemnation. If someone hears we go to church or believe in Jesus, they automatically stereotype us with every attribute they fear from the long list of misperceptions they have about Christians.

When I was a kid, I had a paper route. The pay was lousy, but the tips made the job worthwhile. I went the extra mile to get the paper right on the doormat nice and early. People responded well, and I got pretty good tips. The way *The Sacramento Bee* collected their subscription fees back then was by sending the poor little paperboys door-to-door to say, "Collecting for the paper." This was tedious, sometimes taking numerous trips just to collect from one house.

I'll never forget two houses on my route. One customer was a single guy who lived at what I called "The Party House." He was often hanging out with his friends and always throwing a party.

The other memorable house had Christian signs all over the outside. Christian bumper stickers covered the back of their cars, and the doormat even read, "The Son is Always Shining Here." But I never got a tip from "The Son-Shine House," as I began to call it. As a matter of fact—they were the worst people I had to collect from on my paper route. They always asked if I could come back. Sometimes I would even hear them come to the door, peek out the peephole, and then not answer the door.

One time around Christmas, when tips were always better, I went back to "The Son-Shine House" for the fourth or fifth time to try to collect payment for the last month's bill. I had collected in full from everyone else on the route. Persistence was the only method that seemed to work, so I made a habit of stopping there whenever I passed the house. This particular time I was heading somewhere with my family, and I talked my mom into stopping so I could give it yet another try. Behold—the door opened, and there was the Son-Shine Lady (that's what my brother and I called her).

"Collecting for the paper." (*Again*, I wanted to say!)

"Didn't I already pay?"

"No, ma'am, here's the receipt stub."

She looked over the receipt book. Hers was the only one that wasn't torn from the book. "It seems like you just collected!"

No, I thought, *That was just me knocking and you hiding behind the door!*

"How much?"

"$8.50."

Regretfully, the Son-Shine Lady went and got a $10 bill. The most common tip I received was $1.50. I think this was because it was easy to hand me $10 and get on with life. Some people, particularly the older ones, wanted their two quarters back so they could tip me that even dollar, and an occasional few only tipped me 50 cents. I think that is why I remember this day so clearly.

When she handed me the $10, I did my normal routine: reaching into my pocket, obviously digging out the change, and waiting for the person to say, "Don't worry about it" or "Just keep the change." Well, at this house I kept digging, and the lady just stood there with her hand outstretched. I pulled out a dollar and handed it to her. And then I did the digging motion again while waiting for her line. But her hand stayed out, so I kept digging. I hadn't planned to make this stop, so it was lucky I even had a dollar and some change on me. Unfortunately, as I pulled out my change, I saw that I only had two dimes.

I said, "I only have 20 cents." This would mean she could take the 20 cents, tip me a measly 30 cents, and be done with it.

But she said, "That's okay."

I thought, *Whew, we're done!*

Until she gave back the one-dollar bill, took her ten, and said, "You can come back later."

I always remember that the Son was never shining in that house.

In sharp contrast to the Son-Shine Lady was Party House Guy, whom I had collected from the week before this happened. When I knocked on his door, it opened, blaring loud music and voices. The guy came to the door with a beer in his hand and a girl on his arm.

"Collecting for the paper."

"Oh s--t, yeah I forgot—just a second." He dug into his pocket and pulled out a 20.

I did my typical maneuver, reaching into my pocket to pull out $10 first, hoping that while I was reaching for the rest he would say, "Keep the change." And I barely got my hand in my pocket when he waved his hand and said, "F---in' A. Merry Christmas. Keep the tip." He smiled and closed the door.

Which person do you think I, a 15-year-old kid, wanted to be like?

The Fine Television Example

Years ago I had the privilege of introducing Kristin, an eighth-grade girl, to a relationship with Christ. A few afternoons later I got a phone call.

"Jonathan, it's Kristin."

"Hey Kristin, what's up?"

"Quick! Turn on your TV to channel 10."

"What's up?"

"Just turn it on—it's Ricki Lake. You need to see something. Call me back."

I turned on the TV and switched it to channel 10. Ricki Lake had some special guests on her show—a "Christian" preacher and several people who were living the "homosexual lifestyle." The preacher was in the middle of a huge speech. He was quoting scripture about God's judgment and anger against homosexuals. Then he said something like, "And your lifestyle is an abomination. For that you are going to burn in the eternal flame!"

One of the homosexual individuals responded, "And all I see out of you is hate. If that's what your God is about, then I don't want any of him!"

The crowd clapped furiously.

I sadly dialed Kristin back. She answered quickly.

"That old guy...I'm not what he is, am I?"

Wow! I'll never forget Kristin's question.

The unchurched don't recognize the difference between us and these extreme examples I've just described. In their minds we might be that "Bible Thumper" or that radical who doesn't really represent Christ. Hypocrites exist, and they don't make our job any easier. That's our first thought. But upon further examination, our *own* hypocrisy makes our job just as hard, if not harder.

Who's Our Neighbor?

Ever think about why Jesus told the story of the Good Samaritan? Do you think it was to teach us to care for those who have been beaten up? So many of us miss the true punch of that story. Samaritans were hated by the Jewish people of the day. You see, the true Jews were from the line of Judah, one of Jacob's (Israel's) sons. Most of the other descendants of Israel intermarried with the Gentiles (non-Jews). Some of these descendants were called Samaritans, and the Jews thought they were dirty, godless people.

Jesus told the story of the Good Samaritan to a group of Jews. Picture this: Jesus tells the story of a man who is mugged and left on the road to die. In the story, a priest and a Levite pass by on the other side of the road. The Jews who were listening to this story probably agreed that this would happen because the Levites and priests were bound by the law to ceremonial cleanliness that prohibited them from being in contact with a stranger. The story goes on to tell of a third man who happened by. The Jews were probably already finishing the story in their heads. "Yes, the third man, like a good Jew, will stop and take care of him in a neighborly fashion."

But here's where Jesus switched gears. Jesus chose a Samaritan to be the hero of the story. Jesus tells how the Samaritan stopped and helped this man, bandaged his wounds, and paid for his lodging and care. The punch of this story exists in the fact that the audience, the Jews, couldn't get past the fact that Jesus messed up a perfectly good story by making a Samaritan the hero. They wouldn't even say the word *Samaritan* when Jesus asked them who had acted neighborly.

Jesus cut right to the issue of why the Jews didn't know how to act neighborly. It wasn't because they wouldn't stop on the road to help a poor chap in need; it was because they hated Samaritans.

We, like those particular Jews, are hypocrites. It's so easy to point the finger at others and rest the blame there, but the truth is we *all* need Jesus.

Do You Know That You Don't Know?

A huge problem is that many of us don't even know that we don't understand the unchurched. The more unaware we are of this, the bigger the chasm that separates us from the point of ever reaching them.

During college I worked at a bank. One of my coworkers, Katrina, became a good friend of mine. Katrina is black, and I'm a Scotch-Irish-American mutt. My family wasn't prejudiced at all, and I had been raised to believe that all people are equal, regardless of race, gender, or ability. Growing up I had a lot of friends of different races, and I never thought I really even noticed race or color.

One day while I was working at the bank, my eyes were opened. Katrina and I talked a lot at work, especially during slow days. On this particular day we had a lot of time to converse, and somehow the subject of racism came up. Katrina never brought it up—she was a peacemaker and extremely easy to get along with. In this conversation I was expressing my anger against those who discriminate because of color or make demeaning statements.

Katrina commented, "Most people don't even realize when they're being condescending."

I thought that was really interesting. I asked her for an example. She told me that I made statements like that all the time. I was shocked. Not because Katrina was telling me this—Katrina was cool, and we were friends. She had earned the right to tell me if I had stuck my foot in my mouth. The reason I was shocked was because I literally had no idea what she was talking about.

"Give me an example," I asked.

"The other day you asked me for a comb. I pulled my pick out of my purse, joking with you that it was all I had. You said, 'No, a normal comb!'"

I was dumbfounded. I'd never considered what that sounded like. Now that I thought about it, it did sound pretty degrading. I probed Katrina, and she gave me several more examples. I felt terrible. I'd never considered Katrina to be less than myself; yet in my own ignorance I routinely made degrading remarks around her.

That day I learned that I looked at the world through Caucasian, middle-class, Christian, California-raised eyes. In my mind, *I* was normal. Anyone who didn't fit into these categories was "other" than me, and therefore "other" than normal.

Identify and Eliminate

That day I learned the hard way that I had to make a determined effort to try to understand and consider others with eyes that went beyond what I saw and knew. That day I realized that my actions were based on my own limited perception. If I was going to relate well with others, I needed to identify those areas of ignorance and eliminate the bad habits I had built around these misconceptions.

This book focuses on understanding a group that most of us who have been raised in the church don't understand. This group is the unchurched—people who don't know what "washed in the blood" means, people who can't sing "The Old Rugged Cross" without cracking a hymn book. Often we treat these unchurched people the way I treated Katrina. Sure, we claim they're our friends and that we treat them fine. Yet we make statements like I made to Katrina without even realizing it. It's these kinds of statements that we need to identify and eliminate.

Most people will question me at this point. Most people will say, "Jonathan, I have tons of non-Christian friends and none of them feel awkward around me." Well, some people are better than others, but let me share four major roadblocks that hinder most of us from reaching the unchurched. They cause us to reach *no one* with the life-changing message of Jesus Christ.

Four Roadblocks to Reaching Our Friends

1. Act condescendingly toward them or belittle them.

Some of you might think you don't act this way. I know I thought I didn't. As in the situation with Katrina, I wasn't even aware I did it! See if you can identify with any of these common examples:

Referring to them as "non-Christians." This is something that many of us in the church do. Ironically, even in this book I have consistently referred to them as the "unchurched," a common label we use for this group of people we need to reach. But what if we are in a conversation with them? Do we call them non-Christians? "You don't go to church? I didn't know you were a *non-Christian.*"

Think about the word *non-Christian*. Or better yet, think of it another way. What if someone came up to you and asked you a question you couldn't answer, then politely remarked, "Oh, that's right. You're a non-Buddhist." You'd probably think, *A non-Buddhist? What do you mean a non-Buddhist? Like I would even want to be a Buddhist?*

Get my point? Calling someone a "non" anything assumes they should be that thing. *Non-Christian* is an egotistical word. Even if we truly believe others should be Christians, we're not going to get anywhere by being that condescending toward them.

Using the phrase: "I don't date non-Christians." What does that imply? I've heard this phrase used millions of times in church youth groups. It's a great principle but a lousy way to say it. While it's a good idea for young girls and guys who have Jesus as the number-one priority in their lives to only date others who share that same priority, the phrase "I don't date non-Christians" is a condescending statement. There are better ways to express your dating standards.

Picture this: Randy really wants to ask out Christine. Randy doesn't go to church; and if he's like most students in the beginning of the 21st century, his parents were forced to go to church by their parents, so they vowed never to do that to their children. That's why we have a majority of youth who don't go to church today, except maybe for a funeral or perhaps an occasional Easter service to show off their fancy duds.

When Randy asks Christine to go out with him on Friday night, Christine says, very politely, "I don't date non-Christians." Get into Randy's head for a minute. What is he thinking? First, he's probably confused. The word *Christian* is highly misused, and Randy probably doesn't know what it means. He might even think *he* is a Christian because, after all, America is a Christian nation, right? Chances are when Randy was six or seven years old and some of the kids in school were talking about religion, Randy probably asked his parents what he was, and they most likely told him he was a Christian because he isn't Buddhist, Hindu, or one of those guys in the airport selling flowers.

Not only does Randy probably think he is Christian, but he's probably also wondering why Christine thinks he *isn't*. *Does she think she's too good for me? We've got a regular Mother Teresa here! I don't want to go out with her hypocritical kind anyway!*

Christine could say it another way. She could decline but return the invitation by asking if he would like to go to church or youth group with her. She might even get him to go. Dating only Christians is a great principle I heartily endorse. We just need to be careful how we communicate it.

Respond with "I don't drink." This is just like the phrase about dating. Regardless of their religious views, no teenagers should be drinking alcohol because it's against the law. But what if someone invited you to a party, and there was obviously going to be drinking going on there?

Jimmy comes up to Ryan and asks him, "Are you going to the four-kegger at Megan's this weekend?"

Ryan replies, "I don't drink." Ryan might as well say, "I don't drink like *you* do—you alcoholic scumbag!"

Many of us have great convictions about issues of purity in our lives. But the minute we vocalize them in a way that puts others down, we close doors to ministry. Jesus was always being criticized for hanging out with sinners. In one particular passage (Matthew 9:10-13), Jesus is eating with Matthew and a bunch of his "non-Christian" tax collector friends. All these religious people asked, "Why does Jesus eat with such scum?" Jesus replied something like this: "Healthy people don't need a doctor—sick people do...I have come to help sinners, not those who think they are already good enough."

We need to be careful about what statements we make. Why? Because otherwise we will hit the second roadblock in reaching the unchurched.

2. Eat your words.

Nobody intentionally eats his words or sticks her foot in her mouth (although I wonder sometimes). But many of us have done it at one time or another.

In high school I had a friend who made a stand like we just discussed: "I don't date non-Christians!" She would say it proudly, and it would become a heated discussion in the cafeteria where she ended up looking like a snob. But to make matters worse, she ended up eating her words.

After lunch she and I had English class together. Every Monday there was a vocabulary test in this class. Half the students never bothered studying for the test because it was so easy to cheat, thanks to the clueless teacher who would leave the room while we were taking it. One girl in the class actually printed out tiny definitions of the words on small cheat sheets and passed them around the class. And one day my good friend asked for one of the sheets as they were being passed around. An individual who was at the lunch table not an hour before and had heard her declaration noticed this irony. After class he made a huge spectacle of the "Christian" who wouldn't _date_ a "non-Christian" yet would accept a cheat sheet from one.

As I shared with you earlier, I fell victim to the same situation when I got caught cheating in biology class just a few weeks after "standing up for my faith" and speaking out against evolution. And there were many other times when I would get into some sort of trouble with my mouth or actions, and I was sure to have an audience of "non-Christians" there to point it out to me.

The unchurched, the partiers, the atheists, and anyone who doesn't believe in Jesus think we're all hypocrites. And you know what? They're right! We are. Sometimes we make it harder for people to believe, not only because we mess up, but also because we've either spoken or acted proudly or condescendingly to a group that was just waiting for us to eat our words!

3. Righteously confront those who are wrong.

For years I volunteered in a youth group that was filled with students who wanted to reach their friends with the gospel. Many of them were making a huge impact on their campus and bringing a good number of friends with them to church. There were others who, although their motives were good, used poor discernment regarding how to reach their friends. More often than not these students repelled others from ever thinking about a relationship with God.

One day in youth group these students were sharing about opportunities they had to be a light in this dark world. One of the students stood up and shared an opportunity he had to "reach his friends." He said, "I was sitting in class one day, and I heard these guys talking about parties. They talked about the last party they'd been to and how much beer was there. Then they talked about how much beer and how many 'fine ladies' were going to be at the next party. I stood up and walked over to them and said, 'Hey! You guys are doing wrong! You need to stop that partying and drinking and go to church. Jesus doesn't want you doing that—so stop!' Then I sat down."

I asked him later how effective this little talk was. He said, "They just laughed at me, but that was to be expected from their kind."

I asked this young spitfire a question: "Where in the Bible do you see this kind of rebuking happening?"

He quickly retorted, "Jesus rebuked people all the time."

I asked him again, "Who was Jesus usually rebuking?"

He thought a while this time. "All kinds of people, but usually the Pharisees."

I asked him to share with me just one passage of Scripture where Jesus yelled at and condemned a "non-Christian." He couldn't name one instance because Jesus never did!

So many people like to quote verses about rebuking or correcting. Look at the contexts of these verses; they speak of rebuking and correcting believers, religious people, or false teachers. And Paul actually teaches the opposite approach regarding unbelievers. "What business is it of mine to judge those outside the church? Are you not to judge those inside? God will judge those outside" (1 Corinthians 5:12-13).

Victoria L. B. Hamilton, a senior at duPont Manual High School, shared her feelings about this in an article called "A Question of Faith" in *The Courier Journal.*

> I'm not Christian. My parents...converted to Buddhism. I was born in 1984, so I was born into the religion. When I was growing up, I grew up next door to a Christian minister [who] didn't really want his grandchildren playing with me, and he told them to tell me that I was going to hell. That's just the stigma that I grew up with. [So] I didn't want to talk about religion" (March 16).

Jesus showed us that we're supposed to love the sinner. One of many biblical examples is the story about the adulteress who was caught in the act (John 8). The snobs were really trying to trap Jesus, and they decided to do it at the expense of someone they considered unimportant—a sinner.

Somehow they caught this woman in the act of adultery. (How do you do that? Open random doors and check for wedding rings?) Then they brought her before Jesus and accused her. But where was the man? Religious law, which they knew well, required that *both* parties be stoned (Leviticus 20:10; Deuteronomy 22:22).

Jesus was teaching at the temple courts at the time. Now picture being at church or in class one morning when a bunch of guys burst in holding a woman wrapped in a sheet. We actually don't know what she was wearing—if she was naked or if they gave her a chance to put something on. But you can bet she wasn't in her Sunday best, and it was definitely a bad hair day.

All of these religious snobs probed Jesus and tried to get him to decide the fate of this woman. They had Jesus in a catch-22—if Jesus said they shouldn't stone her, they could accuse him of violating the Mosaic law. But if he told them to stone her, they could report him to the Romans who did not allow the Jews to carry out their own executions.

Jesus did something very cool. Instead of worrying about his own backside, he showed extreme compassion. As the snobs continued to demand an answer—and as the crowd stared at this woman with hateful, judgmental eyes—Jesus bent down and started writing in the dirt. Everyone's focus, which had been on this woman, now shifted to Jesus. The crowd started to look at what Jesus was writing. As the tension built to an unbearable level, Jesus stood and spoke for the first time.

"Go ahead and stone her—but let the person who's never sinned throw the first stone." All the leaders stared at each other. Fists were clenched, rocks were grasped tightly, and glances were exchanged as they waited for something—anything. Perhaps they looked to a leader in their group for assurance, for a first move, an endorsement of their actions to move them on to the next level. But the Bible says the oldest person in the group dropped his stone first. Everyone else in the group followed their elder's lead until only Jesus and the woman remained.

The story is far from over. The woman's life had just been salvaged. The sound of the first rock hitting the ground was probably the best sound she'd heard in her entire life. However, she was probably still a bit apprehensive because even though the guys with the rocks were gone, she now stood before this man who taught at the temple, commanded attention, and swayed the actions of the leaders of the day. Surely her punishment was about to be declared.

Jesus asked her where her accusers were. Nervous, she answered, "They're all gone." Jesus said, "Then I don't accuse you either." Huge sigh of relief. But Jesus, the man of compassion, saw this woman's emptiness calling out. He saw her desperate need for freedom from the life she was leading. Jesus, in complete love and understanding, said, "Go and sin no more." He might have said it like this, "Leave the life that is dragging you down."

Jesus communicated the same thing to this woman that he communicated to Zacchaeus, Matthew, Mary Magdalene, and every sinner he came across. He clearly communicated this message: "I don't care where you've been, but I care where you're going."

That attitude needs to flow from every breath we exhale. We need to be able to see others as the people Jesus has forgiven—he's given them a clean slate and a fresh start. Jesus didn't come here to condemn but to save (John

3:17). He saved his fiery confrontations for the Pharisees and his compassion for the "unchurched."

4. Make them feel like they don't belong.

Years ago we partnered with a church to reach our community with an outreach event. We brought in a famous athlete whose name alone was a huge draw to the community. The purpose of the event was to bring in the unchurched, the non-Christian, and reach them with the life-changing message of Jesus Christ. The event was held at a large church in our area and was widely publicized. I brought four of my unchurched junior high students to the event. They were excited to see the famous athlete and knew nothing else about the evening.

As they walked into the church, one of the boys asked me where the little water dish by the door was so we could sprinkle ourselves as we entered the room. I assured him there was no water dish, and we didn't need to do any sprinkling. We sat down in the comfortable pew, and the service began with a man in a suit walking on stage. The music started, he grabbed a microphone, and he said, "Everybody knows this one—sing along with me," and he started singing a well-known church song. No words on an overhead, no song sheets, just "Everybody knows this one."

All four of my students looked at each other and shrugged their shoulders. After we sang several "familiar" songs, a guy came up on stage and started talking about how far today's youth are from the church and how much they needed God. I'll never forget how he said, "Do you know how many kids don't even know John 3:16?" My students shrugged again. Then one of them leaned over and asked me if the athlete was coming on soon. I assured him it would be soon.

Sure enough, he was going to come up right after—oh no—the offering. The biggest complaint I've heard from the unchurched is, "I don't want to go to church because all they want is my money!" Well, we proved them right that evening. I couldn't help but assume that all the unchurched guests felt like they didn't belong that night.

If you want a roadblock that stops most anyone, make them feel like they don't belong. Speak a language they don't understand. Make them feel stupid for not knowing anything about the Bible or about your church. Bring them to events that reek with the stench of "No non-Christians allowed!"

I'm not saying, "Don't bring kids to church." I brought those same students to my church, and they didn't feel as awkward as they did at that event. They had some preconceived ideas, but they knew we were going to church. I also selected this particular church because it made people feel welcome. It didn't make people feel stupid if they didn't know the church routine. It gave away Bibles to anyone who needed one. And most importantly, before every offering they'd announce, "If this is your first time with us, this offering is not for you. We don't want your money; we're just glad you're here. This is for the people who regularly attend and call this their church home."

5. Run away.

Reaching students isn't going to happen if our actions make them want to run away. We need to be aware of what we say and do, even if we think we're the most seeker-friendly place around.

Understanding the unchurched will pave the way to reaching unchurched youth. Avoiding roadblocks will keep our feet out of our mouths so we can begin to have meaningful conversations with them and build bridges toward sharing our faith.

chapter 6

Reaching...Not Repelling

Developing a
relational approach

Several years ago we had a large event that hundreds of junior high kids attended. A powerful speaker preached the gospel, and a swarm of students came forward to make a commitment to Jesus. The only thing they needed was a counselor to meet with them. But with such a large number coming forward, we didn't have enough counselors. One of our workers spotted two guys he knew from church who happened to be visiting the facility where our event took place. They had been thoroughly trained on how to present the gospel and did an excellent job counseling several students who came forward.

The event ended, and these two counselors strutted outside, ecstatic that they'd had an opportunity to share the gospel. In their excitement they were boldly talking with groups of kids on their way out of the event, asking questions and giving short soliloquies along the way. They came across some of the students I'd brought who were on the way to our van. Several of my students had come forward at the altar call that evening. The students these fellows approached were the students who had *not* gone forward. One of them was Kelly. They asked her, "So—what did you think of tonight?"

"It was all right," she reluctantly answered, exchanging glances with her friends and wondering who these guys were.

"What did you think of the speaker?"

"He's cool."

"What did you think when he gave the opportunity for you to give your life to Jesus?"

Walking faster and trying to end the conversation, Kelly responded, "I don't get into that serious stuff."

"When will it be time for you to get serious?"

"I don't know...I just don't get into it." By now the girls reached the van, opened the door, and scurried inside.

But the two guys stood at the open door of the van and said, "Well, what if time runs out? Like if you were to get into a car accident on the way home tonight? Would you wish you would have gotten serious?"

Kelly was sitting against the far side of the van now, attempting to look out the window the other way. Trying to end the conversation, she said, "I really don't want to talk about this serious stuff right now."

And these two kept talking. By the time I arrived, unfortunately a few minutes behind my group, one of the guys was giving an elaborate illustration of how no one, regardless of how good a jumper they were, could jump across the great chasm that exists between us and God. Kelly and her friends looked like cats cornered in an alley by a stray dog.

I started the van and quickly announced it was time to go. Now the two fellows looked at me as if I had the mark of the Beast on my forehead and tried to continue. I pressed the accelerator anyway, and I'll never forget what Kelly said as we exited the parking lot: "I'll never go to one of these again!"

For years my staff continued loving Kelly and her friends. One of Kelly's friends began a relationship with Jesus about a year later, but we never could break down the walls that Kelly and her other friends had put up.

Timing Is Everything

Someone may know how to present the gospel, she might know all kinds of cool stories and illustrations, and she might even know convincing methods of persuasion. But it doesn't matter how good a presentation someone has to make if she doesn't have any sense of when to make it.

Through more than a decade of marriage, I've learned a lot about listening. Unfortunately I learned most of the lessons the hard way. During the first year of our marriage, my wife, Lori, would come home from a hard day and share a problem she faced. I, being the man with all the answers, was gracious enough to solve those problems for her by explaining what she did wrong and what she needed to do in the future. After several experiences of sleeping on the couch, I eventually realized, "Hey—she doesn't want answers! She just wants someone to *listen* to her!"

Sometimes people just need others to listen to them. Sometimes people just need friends. And being a friend will open the door in God's timing. God will provide a number of opportunities for you to share your faith with your friends, neighbors, and coworkers. Presenting the gospel is easy. Knowing when to do it and finding those open doors is the tough part.

You don't have to know someone to share the gospel. If you want to, you could knock on 100 doors a day with your Bible in your hand, and you could preach the Romans Road to them—not a bad thing at all. But in my years of sharing my faith with the unchurched I've discovered that of those 100 people:

* 50 people won't be home or just won't answer their doors.

* 20 aren't going to let you talk.

* 15 will let you talk for about 30 seconds before they tell you they aren't interested.

* Five are going to listen to everything you say and may even ask you questions. But they're from another religion or cult, and they just want to hear what you have to say so they can try to convince you otherwise.

* Five are going to listen to what you have to say, smile, and then let you know what church they go to and that they're proud of you for doing what you're doing.

* Three are going to listen quickly and then ask if you can leave something with them because they don't want to make any decisions right now.

* Two are going to listen, talk to you, ask sincere questions, and maybe—by God's grace—make a decision for Christ.

If your odds are this good, then there will be a party in heaven that night because two people will come to Christ, maybe more. But what about the hundreds of opportunities God has placed before you with your friends, neighbors, coworkers, and family? Can you just knock on their doors and give some presentation? You have to see these people every day, every week, every month, or every Thanksgiving and Christmas. They have already watched you; eaten with you; talked with you; gossiped with you; seen the way you do things; and know what makes you mad, impatient, bitter—even snobby! How are you going to reach these people?

One of the many things Jesus was really good at doing was building relationships. He cared for people and didn't condemn them for their actions. Yet he was very honest with them about the direction they were heading in their lives. He often met people's physical needs first, which opened the door to meeting their spiritual needs. Jesus was a master at relational evangelism: building a relationship, developing trust, and earning the right to be heard.

Relational evangelism requires a lot of effort and patience. It demands that one key word—*love*. But when an unchurched student is in a bind and needs help, who is she going to turn to? The stranger knocking at the door with an agenda, or the friend they've been having coffee with for the past year?

Three Approaches to Relationship Building

The Aggressive Approach

This one is much like the one I described earlier in this chapter. These people have an agenda, and they feel it's from God. If someone gets in their way or gets hurt—too bad, so sad! Aggressive people never consider another person's feelings. Consequently, they aren't highly relational, and they often have quick "drive-thru" relationships where they clearly present the "turn or burn" message. Aggressive relationships usually end up building walls instead of breaking them down. Unfortunately, aggressive people never see that fact until it's too late.

The Passive Approach

This is the polar opposite of the aggressive approach. These people feel like they need to really get to know a person before they share with them. They will spend months, years, even decades waiting for "just the right time." These people tend to be insecure in their approach. This insecurity or lack of confidence stifles them from sharing. This group's common excuse is not having "the gift of evangelism." But this has nothing to do with spiritual gifts and everything to do with a lack of Spirit-led boldness. People using both the aggressive approach and the passive approach are thinking about their own agendas, not God's.

The Balanced Approach

This approach understands that God wants to reach people, and he wants to use you and me to do it. A person using a balanced approach doesn't beat people over their heads with the Bible yet looks for open doors and creates opportunities to share. The person with the balanced approach is a person who has figured out the secret. If you can figure out the secret, your life will be changed. Do you want to know the secret? Come in really close to the book—I'm going to whisper it: "Get out of the driver's seat and let God drive!" Don't try to do it alone. When we try to do anything on our own, we end up messing it all up anyway. Give God control.

Listen to what great news this is! Most people find evangelism terrifying. Think about it. Think of someone you know who doesn't know Jesus. Now think about trying to talk with him about it. Ninety percent of you just got the willies. *What if I say something wrong? What if I blow it? What if I can't answer that tough question? I'm not worthy!*

God wants to reach people, and he wants to use us to do it. Say that out loud; make it personal. "God wants to reach people, and he wants to use me to do it." Say it again. "God wants to reach people, and he wants to use ME to do it!" God doesn't want you to beat people over the head with a Bible. He doesn't want you to set up an easel in people's living rooms. He doesn't want you to use little sales tricks to trap people into decisions. He wants to reach people, and he wants you to get in on the experience!

Five Relational Guidelines

The balanced approach to relationship building follows three relational guidelines. These guidelines will help you open doors and, more importantly, keep your foot out of your mouth.

1. Develop a sensitive approach.

Many times it's not what you say—it's how you say it. Two women could individually approach Monica, a pregnant teenager, and start asking the exact same questions. One woman could be seen as warm, caring, and truly interested in Monica. The other could be considered pushy, nosy, or come across as a custody lawyer. Two men could come up to Andre, a 25-year-old steel worker who's been around the block, and ask the exact same questions. One man could be received as friendly, casual, and cool. The other could be considered aggressive, nosy, or come across as a parole officer.

Having a conversation with someone is not simply rattling off a list of questions. Set a pace; watch for nonverbal cues. If the person is fidgeting or acting uncomfortable, maybe you're talking too deep, too soon. Know when to back off. A sensitive approach demands patience. It won't lunge for the spiritual jugular in the first five minutes. You're building a relationship—not staging an intervention.

2. Start conversations with "light" content.

I was working with a guy I had just met. We were doing some hard labor off by ourselves, and he started a conversation with me. "Jonathan, do you ever struggle with masturbation?" I burst out laughing, thinking he was joking. He wasn't; he wanted to talk about it. It was a very awkward conversation. I spent the whole conversation trying to escape. This guy is not my choice invite for a Sunday barbeque. Why? Because he starts conversations with probing content. Immediately my walls go up, and I jump to a defensive mode, not letting anyone come inside.

Conversations with people should be handled the same way small group discussions are handled. Being in ministry, we use small groups as a tool to make people feel comfortable and open up. When writing small group questions, the golden rule is to start with easy questions and slowly get more personal. You wouldn't get into a small group with a bunch of strangers and say, "Everyone share your name and a sin you've committed that you've never told anyone about!" A good opening small group question would be, "Share your name and your favorite restaurant." People like food, and most people have a favorite place to eat. This is a simple question that almost anyone would be comfortable to share.

After some fun simple questions, transitional questions can be introduced. These are light questions that can lead to deeper subjects. "What is the best thing a friend ever did for you?" This question isn't very intimidating and it naturally leads to this question, "What is the worst thing a friend ever did to you?" Now you are introducing more personal questions. These aren't questions you would start with, but now that you've led up to them, a person should feel more comfortable about responding. Which leads us to our next guideline.

3. Get permission to ask deeper or more intimate questions.

You might see someone for only a few minutes a day on a bus or at the copy machine. After a week of small talk and then slowly talking about more personal stuff, it won't be awkward to simply ask her, "Do you mind if I ask you a question?" Sure, you've already been asking some questions, but this prepares her for the more intimate ones. This also helps set a pace for later when you might ask her if you can share something important—and then share the gospel.

One thing we need to remember, though, is that this process doesn't necessarily happen in just one conversation. Slowly, you are building bridges. We will talk about every stage of this process in chapter 8, "Building Bridges."

4. Don't use trickery.

Some churches and organizations train their people to use trickery to try to open the door to talk to people. They don't call it trickery, but it's a backdoor approach to sharing the gospel. This sales approach is definitely in the aggressive realm.

We had some good friends who invited us over for dinner one evening, and we gladly accepted. While getting ready to leave for their house that evening, my son became extremely sick. We ended up having to cancel. This friend of mine said, "Oh, don't worry about it; they'll be doing it again sometime."

I didn't understand what he said, and being as assertive as I am, I asked, "I'm sorry—*they* will be doing it again? Who are 'they'?"

He stumbled and realized he had slipped. "Uh, the people that—well the people from…" and he named the multilevel marketing company they were working for.

I quickly replied, "Oh, I'm embarrassed. I thought you just invited us over for dinner as friends. I'm sorry I misunderstood!"

We got off the phone, and I was steamed. I had never been so glad that my son was sick! If you've ever had an easel set up in your living room by a friend or if you've ever met with a friend to supposedly talk with him about something important and you were told about a "great business opportunity," then you know what I was feeling. This is not the kind of technique you want to use to build relationships or to share your faith.

I've seen gospel tracts that were a copy of a $20 bill on one side with a gospel message printed on the other side. I actually knew people who left those as tips, justifying this by saying they were furthering the kingdom. There is no better way to make a waitress hate "Christians" than to stiff her with a gospel tract. This method closes doors and builds walls, as all methods of trickery do.

5. Understand gender lines.

Adults Reaching Youth

When an adult is ministering to youth (someone besides her own children), she should always target the same gender. I don't know how many times I've seen this line crossed. And I've also seen staff members fired, lawsuits filed, and in the worst cases—kids abused or taken advantage of. Adults should never hang out with students of the opposite sex. Crushes can develop—or even worse, adults can fall for a young girl or boy. Hanging out with the opposite sex can also create competition with youth of the same sex, who will now see us as competition both relationally and sexually. And that means doors to reach the same sex, the doors we *should* be targeting, are now closed.

Students Reaching Students

Student leaders should also adhere to these boundaries. I taught a session on reaching your friends for Christ, and I remember a girl coming up to me and several staff members afterward. She asked for advice on how to share Christ with the two non-Christian guys she had brought with her to the camp. I listened for a while to make sure I understood the situation.

The night before she had stayed up until 2 a.m. talking with one of the guys, sharing her heart for God. I asked if she was dating either of them. She said that she had no dating interest in either of them and that she was trying to make that clear. I had seen her earlier that evening sitting with the two of them, and one of them was hanging all over her, resting his head on her shoulder, and so on. The guy clearly had a crush on her and was hoping he had a shot at something a little more serious with her. She wasn't giving him that, and now he was acting cold around her. She didn't understand why.

I explained to her a little about guys. I affirmed her great motives, staying up until 2 a.m. to share with him. However, this guy's motives, perhaps pure in the beginning, were probably swayed as the evening went on. Although it might not be fun to admit, guys are very vulnerable to sexual temptations. Their sex drives often get in the way. When even the nicest of guys is spending alone time with a girl who is "just a friend," he will be mentally distracted by his hormones and will often be plagued with what I call "tunnel vision."

Tunnel vision is a mode that guys get into, often late at night, when they disregard better judgment for the quick thrill of the moment. Guys can even get in this mode with girls who aren't that attractive to them, although it's not something they'd like to admit. When a guy has tunnel vision, he'll appear to be a real sweetheart because he is using every piece of ammo he has to get what he wants. If a girl walks away from one of these situations without an incident of any kind occurring, she will often have no idea what went on because she assumed the guy had the same motives she did: companionship, good conversation, and friendship.

Unfortunately, many Christians don't address this. They try to sweep it under the rug. But we can't ignore the fact that historically, men have thrown away their marriages, their careers, their whole lifestyles for a few minutes of fun. That's why accountability is so necessary for men. That's why wise men like Billy Graham won't ride in an elevator alone with any woman other than his wife. Men need to be aware of this weakness, and women need to beware.

Adults Reaching Adults

When adults are reaching adults, this "target your own gender" guideline isn't as clear-cut. Very often a woman can convince a man, who never would have considered doing it otherwise, to go to church. But there are still plenty of problems. What happens when he is only in it for her and doesn't care about God? What if she falls for him, and he still doesn't want a relationship with God? A relationship exists, but trouble is brewing.

Red Flags

Let me just say this: When reaching the opposite sex, a lot of red flags exist, especially with teenagers reaching teenagers. I don't recommend "evangelistic dating." There's a lot of potential for backfire, as reaching the opposite sex flirts with a lot of volatile feelings. And relationships involve enough confusion and emotion without adding an unbalanced spiritual element to the situation.

We don't need to be cloistered away from the opposite sex, but we do need to be careful. We need to remember to "throw off everything that hinders and the sin that so easily entangles, and let us run with perseverance the race marked out for us" (Hebrews 12:1).

Sharing our faith is more than what we say—it's how we say it. The way we build relationships will dictate how many doors will be opened to us. We have an incredible message to share and an incredible motivation to share it. Remember—God wants to reach people, and he wants to use us to do it.

chapter 7

Finding Frames

Communicating in a language
they understand

A typical campus is made up of various social groups, each filled with completely different students. One group might be known as skaters and recognized by a certain attitude and dress. Another group might be the football players with an entirely different outlook and demeanor. But just around the corner is a small group of guys who are playing chess and talking about the Mathletes competition after school. The groups don't end here; there are plenty more. And does a single approach reach all these students?

We all see the world through certain frames. And we also frame all of the messages that attempt to enter our brains. Frames are the lenses through which we see the world around us. Our education, background, ethnicity, experiences, tragedies, desires, hobbies, and friends can all be frames. They affect how we interpret life experiences. They affect how we hear what we hear. They even affect how we look at ourselves. If the message is outside our frame, we often don't hear it. If the message fits one of our frames, we not only hear it, but we also understand the message and the implications.

And when we share Christ with others, they are looking at our message through their own frames and bringing into the conversation their own presuppositions and assumptions. In order to get to know students so we can eventually communicate Christ with them, we have to figure out what kind of frames they have and then communicate using those frames.

Every one of the students in these groups around campus has different frames. Every person has different experiences, reactions, and thoughts that all contribute to a unique set of frames. So how do we reach such diverse youth? Can't we just bring in a band and a speaker to reach all of them?

My dad tells the story of when he was shopping for an RV some years back. As he and my mom shopped around, they "framed" their RV shopping experience by two criteria. First, they wanted an RV to camp in the woods. They like to visit national parks and wanted a motor home that could take them there. My dad also had this picture that he would be able to get away from his office and spend a great deal of time writing his next book or doing research. My mom is a college professor and is with students and faculty all week long. For her, the idea of getting away from people for some quiet time to do some reading sounded inviting. Perhaps an RV was the way to go.

The second criteria to their buying frame was a financial principle they both have followed their entire lives. They pay cash for purchases that depreciate. For their cars, furniture—you name it—they like to pay cash. The only debt they feel okay about having is real estate, which usually appreciates.

When my parents walked into an RV show, the salesman immediately started talking to them about the benefits of buying an RV. That was the first mistake. He started by talking! He emphasized that what they would love most about RVing is meeting other RVers. He described the RV parks where people get together each evening, visit, and have a lot of fun together. I can picture the look on my parents' faces. He was not appealing to their frame at all. My dad was looking for a place to be alone in nature, and he probably was beginning to wonder if the RV was really for him or not.

It got worse. As this salesman stepped into each RV, he would say, "Tom and Susie, for only $350 a month you can have this model today and be in an RV park meeting other RVers this weekend!"

The sad thing about this story is that my parents would have been so easy to frame. They knew exactly what they wanted and how they were going to pay for it. But this salesperson was delivering a message that was framed by his desires. Not once did he ask my parents what *they* were looking for or what *they* wanted to use the RV for. He had not framed them as they walked into the RV show.

In some ways we can turn off the people around us the same way some salespeople do. Too many sales pitches are salesperson-framed instead of customer-based, where the salesperson believes in the product and goes on and on about it without ever discovering the buyer's needs or wants.

If we are going to get involved in unchurched students' lives, we need to be interested in more than what we are "selling." We need to discover where the other person is coming from. We need to learn the art of framing.

Three Steps to Framing

1. We need to find their frames.

If we are going to impact unchurched students, first we need to figure out their frames. The best way to do this is through research, observation, and asking questions.

The fact that you are reading this book means you already took the first step. The beginning of this book is research into the mind of the unchurched. You can continue researching current trends and philosophies on the World Wide Web. Our ministry—www.TheSourceForYouthMinistr y.com—always has articles, interviews, ideas, and resources that help youth workers reach today's youth. One of our most popular pages is our "Teen Lingo" page, a dictionary of current terms and phrases used by today's generation. You can learn what a "bang" is or what "420" means on this page. YouthSpecialties.com also has a ton of great articles and resources dealing with today's youth and how to reach them.

Check out www.CPYU.org for the latest in statistics and facts about today's youth culture. Walt Mueller provides free resources like his CPYU e-update to keep you current.

But don't stop with just research. Observation is essential. Go on campuses and to sports events. Go wherever kids hang out. Do something that very few adults do—just notice them. Notice what they wear, what they talk about, and what they do. Notice how they talk to each other, their topics of conversation, their opinions and beliefs.

You can only go so far with observation before you have to ask some questions. Questions—and how to ask them—are so important that we devote an entire chapter of this book to them. But as we saw in the example of the RV salesman above, questions are the essential tool that many of us forget to use. How are we to discover others' frames if we don't ask them any questions?

At the beginning of this chapter, I painted the picture of a campus filled with groups of students. Each of these groups has its own telltale signs and characteristics. And many of these characteristics are obvious to the onlooker: body piercings, thick makeup, skateboards, football jerseys, tight clothes, baggy clothes, shaved heads, long hair, and so on. But sometimes the deeper characteristics aren't painted on their faces: loneliness, grief, fear, hopelessness, emptiness, confusion, and regret. Questions are a way for us to start with the external observations and then begin to peel back the layers to discover students' frames. Questions can also help us achieve the second step of framing—finding common ground.

2. We need to find common ground.

In the discovery step of framing, we gather information. Now we take that information and line up our frames to theirs.

One summer I volunteered with a junior high group at my church. Every Tuesday night they had a pool party at someone's house. I remember pulling up to the house my first week. I didn't know anyone, not a single kid. I was actually sweating.

As I walked into the backyard, I observed many different groups of kids. There were some hyper, wiry kids fighting over a rubber ball in the pool. There were some bigger "cool" kids slamming basketballs into a floating hoop in the shallow end. Six or seven girls huddled together in the hot tub area, whispering and watching the guys playing basketball. A slightly overweight kid with swim goggles fixed tightly around his head wandered around the outside of the pool, trying to decide what he was going to do. More girls sat around a staff girl over by the house, and a group of small boys were all hanging off a big staff member.

I settled into a chair in the corner and began to observe. I quickly picked out that some of the kids playing basketball weren't using words that would secure a PG rating. They didn't seem to be worried about anyone else in the pool, and their attention never strayed from the hoop. It wasn't long before they tired of the pool and made their way to the front driveway. I moseyed out front and blended in behind a welcome table bustling with staff people. After a few minutes I saw them finish a game of three on three, and I decided to make my move.

I walked up to the six kids and said, "Which one of you is the best shot?"

About three of the guys started claiming that they were the best, replaying some of the highlights of the prior game. Smiling, I offered my own observations about the last game.

"I don't know...I think Cameron has a pretty good outside shot."

Cameron glowed. He threw his arms in the air like the victor.

Then I offered my proposal, "You wanna find out who's best?"

They all looked at me for the answer. I continued, "Do you guys know how to play knockout?"

Before they had a chance to answer, I explained to them how the game worked. Everybody lines up at the free-throw line and tries to shoot the ball in before the guy behind them.

We played a few rounds, and I won the second round. (This was God's grace because I stink at hoops!) The whole time I played, I learned their names and interacted with them. By round three I thought I'd try something else.

"Hey, that's two in a row. I bet you all a milkshake that I can beat you all again." They all stuck their hands out, ready to bet.

One kid asked skeptically, "What? You'll buy each of us a milkshake if you lose?"

I smiled. "Yep. If I win, you *all* pitch in and buy me one milkshake. But if you win, I have to buy EACH of you a milkshake at the fast-food place of your choice."

All the kids looked at each other like they had been offered gold! "Deal!"

They beat the snot out of me in that next game. I think I was the first one out. And guess what? I had to take them all out for milkshakes.

Through that experience I found out that two of them didn't even go to the church. They just came with their friend to the pool parties. That's why I told them I'd pick them up after youth church on Sunday. All six of them went to youth church that week, and by one o'clock I was sitting in a booth and, sucking down a milkshake with a $15 dent in my wallet.

I didn't know much about them. But I knew they liked basketball, and they all liked milkshakes. So that's where I started.

Imagine a picture frame without a picture in it, hanging on a yardstick in front of your head. The yardstick is protruding from your forehead, and at the end of it is your communication frame. When you listen, see, and communicate, you do it all through that frame. It is your frame of reference for all of your understanding and communication. And when two people are communicating, they must line up those two frames. Without that alignment, there is no communication.

If I walked up to those boys in the pool and started playing the accordion, asking, "Who wants to square dance?" most of you would agree that I probably wouldn't have any success. That's pretty obvious. But sometimes we try very similar approaches with the unchurched. We don't seek common ground. We assume that if we get a band, our Friday-night event will be a success. We assume that if we play games, kids will enjoy our Wednesday-night program. We assume that if we walk up to a kid on campus, he wants to talk to us.

We need to spend time finding common ground. As we research, observe, and question, we can find common ground that might just start us out on the right foot for building relationships. Framing is just a tool we use in building relationships. We'll learn much more about building relational bridges in later chapters.

3. We need to adjust our message to their frames.

Now that our frames are lined up, we can communicate in a language they understand.

Notice that communicating our message to them is the last step. We only move toward the gospel in a conversation after we have researched, observed, and questioned in order to discover their frames. Through this process of discovery, we find common ground to communicate.

This doesn't mean trying to be something we're not. I always remember a teacher I had in junior high who thought he was "just one of the guys." He would walk up to a crowd of kids and say, "Hey, what's going down!" with high fives and special handshakes. Students would smile and make conversation, but after he left, they would laugh at him. One time a cool kid in the group even said, "We should at least give him a break and act nice to him. He's trying!"

The teacher would always wander over to the group during lunch or after school. He would monopolize the conversation and offer advice readily. I don't remember his ever asking a question. The group always humored him—but they never let him in.

Adjusting our message doesn't mean talking like MTV hosts or getting multiple body piercings. Adjusting our message means taking what we've discovered about people and using that as a springboard for conversation.

I'll never forget a time when I *didn't* do this. I worked for a nonprofit at the time, and I was meeting with a huge donor to our organization. We depended on donors like him. So I immediately started pitching a need we had for monthly giving to our ministry. He squirmed in his chair for a few moments before interrupting me, saying, "I'm really not interested in giving on a monthly basis."

Wow. Rejection.

I hadn't framed him. He was a cut-to-the-chase kind of guy. He was excited about ministry projects, not paying someone's salary. He liked to give special gifts, not monthly amounts. It wasn't until I really sat down and talked with him that I realized this. I had spoken too soon.

During the rest of our meeting I listened to his passions and his heart for ministry. And afterward I had a pretty clear idea of his frame. Three months later I was raising funds for a van to bring kids to church. I called him up and met with him. After listening to him for a while, I made a one-minute presentation. I said, "Mike, I know your time is valuable so I'll get right to the point. We have more kids who want to go to church each week than we can take. We've checked out our options, and the best one is a 15-passenger van. I've priced three of them, and they all seem to be around $20,000 for a slightly used one. I hoped you would pray and see what God lays on your heart to do."

Mike committed to do so, and by the end of the month I had a $5,000 dollar check in my hand. This was the same guy I'd met with three months prior and asked to make a commitment to give $100 a month.

We make the same mistakes in our ministry. We often try one method or one message and expect results. We don't see the students' actions as opportunities for discovery—we see them as obstacles. Then our message misses them, and we wonder why.

"Heck, we've always just had Bible study in the youth room on Wednesday night! These students just don't have any desire to get into God's Word! I'm not responsible for their demise!"

"Kids today just don't respect adults. I've told those neighborhood kids a million times not to ride their skateboards on the church grounds. Can't they read the signs? One of them is going to fall and break their neck, and our church is going to get sued. What then?"

"Those kids over there are smoking. I don't think we need that kind of element around our Christian kids. I don't want to sit around and watch them kill themselves!"

If we spend time discovering their frames, we can find common ground and adjust our message. We can discover why they don't want to attend a Wednesday-night Bible study. Maybe if we listened to this group we would discover that they don't think the Bible has any answers for their problems. But they would love an arena where they felt safe to share their problems and look for answers. If we "adjusted our message" by adjusting our method, then Wednesday nights could turn into small group nights. After listening to the students, we come up with the name "Safe House." They like it, and they start bringing their friends. This arena would be a place where the Bible could be shared, and Bible studies could develop from it.

If we spend time discovering their frames and finding common ground, we might discover that kids just want a place to skateboard. After spending time getting to know some of the skaters that come around, we discover that they'd like a place where they can skate without being hassled. So we could "adjust our message" by starting a skate ministry called "No Hassle." We get some ramps, some grinding rails, and one heck of an insurance policy, and we tell every skater we know that No Hassle is at the church on Thursday nights. They skate for an hour, someone shares their testimony for 10 minutes, and then they can skate for 20 more minutes.

If we spend time discovering kids' frames and finding common ground, we might discover that smoking is just one of their vices. They're used to rejection, and they expect it from the church. We "adjust our message," and we don't condemn them. We love them anyway. We accept them and invite them in.

Framing is just a tool to reach diverse youth where they're at. It starts with finding their frames. Once we find common ground, we adjust our message. But now that we understand their frames, how do we go from an everyday conversation to sharing Jesus Christ?

chapter 8

Building Bridges

Moving beyond everyday conversations to sharing the gospel

Lance grew up in a home where God wasn't important. His family never went to church or even discussed the existence of God for that matter. His parents would always tell him, "It doesn't matter what you believe, as long as you're sincere." As Lance got older, he would hear the mention of God, Jesus, heaven, or hell. Every piece of information he received about these subjects would affect how close he would get to knowing Jesus as his personal Lord and Savior.

This process might have started when he was six years old and his first grade friend Steven invited him to a vacation Bible school one summer. Here Lance heard Bible stories for the first time. He even heard something about Jesus loving us all. Maybe Lance didn't hear anything again until a science class in junior high. Here his teacher talked about the earth deriving from a big bang and people being derived from an amino acid that just decided to start living. Maybe Lance readily accepted this as truth.

Then when Lance was in high school, his friend Sean invited him to a ski retreat with his church. Lance heard a speaker talk about the fact that Jesus was the only way to a relationship with God. Sean asked Lance what he thought about the speaker.

Lance said, "It doesn't matter what you believe, as long as you are sincere."

Sean asked him, "Why do you think it matters if you're sincere?"

This disturbed Lance, but he tried not to think any more about it. After all, he was there to ski.

When Lance was a freshman in college, his father died. Lance's friend Michelle was a huge comfort to him during that time. Michelle hung out with Lance off and on for a few weeks and finally shared how God gave her comfort through difficult times in her life. She even prayed with Lance, and he found that comforting.

Two years later Derek, a friend at work, shared the gospel with Lance and asked him if he wanted a relationship with God. Lance, sensing something missing in his life and seeing that God was the answer, gladly turned his life over to Jesus.

Who shared their faith with Lance? Did Derek lead him to Christ? Throughout Lance's life a number of people influenced him: A first grader named Steven simply invited him to vacation Bible school, his friend Sean invited him on the ski trip and talked with him briefly, Michelle was able to encourage Lance and show a genuine reflection of God's love, and then Derek shared the gospel. Who shared their faith with Lance?

Is sharing our faith just a proposal that we give? Many of us think of sharing our faith as an event we can do in a given number of minutes. This limits us in our thinking. Sharing our faith is actually a process. Furthermore, we might be only part of this process. The fact is, each individual had a small part in the process of God drawing Lance to him. "No one can come to me unless the Father who sent me draws him, and I will raise him up at the last day" (John 6:44).

We need to understand that God might use us as only part of the process. We also need to understand that we aren't called to jump right to the end with any given individual. In other words, we aren't to jump straight from "Hi, how are you?" to "Do you know that God loves you and wants a relationship with you?"

I have always loathed hearing the words, "You have to go to the following training session." Who wants to sit through a seminar? I remember when I was a teenager and I wanted to be a counselor for an evangelism crusade. To be a counselor you had to go to four evening training sessions. The only available time for me was Tuesdays, and that meant missing *The A-Team*, *Riptide*, and *Remington Steele*—bummer!

I remember going to these four sessions, and they weren't bad. They weren't *The A-Team* setting explosions and flipping cars over, but they were tolerable. And they taught us how to share the gospel. I was now more than equipped for the large group event. So when the speaker asked the people who wanted to give their lives to Jesus to come forward, we met them and shared the gospel with them. The training worked great. The people who came forward would tell us something like, "I need Jesus. How can I have him?" And we would gladly tell them how to give their lives to Jesus. I prayed with several people my own age who gave their lives to Jesus, and I was ecstatic.

But then I got to school—now what? I knew how to share the gospel when someone provoked people to respond and come forward to give their lives to Jesus. But no one was coming up to me at school or in my neighborhood and telling me, "Hey, I need Jesus. How can I have him?" It was simple. As long as someone could convince people that their whole lives up to that moment had been foolish and that they needed to stop going in the direction they were headed and turn to God, then—and only then—could I tell them how to do that. Guess what? No one convinced people at my school that they needed to change their lives and start living for God. And no one ever walked up to me and said, "I need Jesus. Tell me how to get him!"

It would be nice if it were that easy. It would be nice if someone would just admit, "I need Jesus; give him to me!" If so, we could just learn how to present the gospel. And knowing how to do that is important—presenting a clear understanding of God's love for us, how we mess it all up, what Jesus did for us, and what we can do about it. I'm going to tell you how to do that later in the book because a lot of us don't know how to do that. But the question I have is—once you know how to present the gospel, how do you get to the opportunity to present the gospel?

Most of us are probably pretty cordial when we see our neighbors at the mailbox. We probably say "Hi!" or "How's the wife and kids?" What if God convinced you that you needed to share the gospel with that neighbor? How would you do it? Let's say you read my chapter on sharing the gospel, or you go to some gospel-sharing training session and you know *how* to present the gospel. Now *when* are you going to do it? Are you going to go outside 365 days a year and wait for your neighbor to be crying at his mailbox so he can look up at you through his tear-filled eyes and say, "I need Jesus—present the gospel to me!" If so, you're going to be waiting a long time. Chances are he's never going to ask you that question.

This chapter is dedicated to the unchurched kids on campus, the fringe kids in your youth group, the guy at the mailbox, the friend at work, your nonbelieving father—the people who aren't coming up and begging you for Jesus. The people you say "hi" to and then talk with about the weather, family, cars, or politics. How do you get to a point where you can share the gospel with them? In other words, how are you going to get from an everyday "Hi, how are you?" to "Can I share something with you?"

You'll find elements in the BRIDGE method that overlap with what we learned in the framing chapter. Building bridges is another way to look at how we can open the door to reach the unchurched.

The BRIDGE Method—BRIDGE the gap of "Hi, how are you?" to "Can I share something with you?"

Begin with God

This step is probably the most neglected step in sharing our faith. Many of us get our own agendas, our own motives, and our own ideas in the way of God's work. Some of us may take a training session and burst out of the starting blocks inspired with the new methods we've learned. Then we gladly stuff it down people's throats without ever being responsive to God's leading. Most of us are just so scared of the thought of sharing our faith that we don't consult God because we're afraid he might ask us to do it.

2 Corinthians 4:7 reads, "But we have this treasure in jars of clay to show that this all-surpassing power is from God and not from us." God's treasure is held in perishable containers or "jars of clay." What should be the focus then—the jars or the treasure?

For my birthday dinner my wife always asks me what I want to eat. I get to choose the main course *and* the dessert—not many celebrations present this opportunity. My main course request varies, but the dessert request rarely changes. My wife makes an incredible banana cream pie, which is not only the most delicious pie you've ever tasted, but it is also a work of art. The whipped cream (we don't settle for meringue) smothers the top and has little waves that rise up, inviting you to dip your finger into one of them for a preview of its delight. Macadamia nuts and small pieces of slightly browned coconut are speckled across the top. It's wonderful! I'm salivating just thinking about it. Every year when my wife brings out the pie, we all marvel at its beauty, eagerly awaiting to partake of its goodness. Not once have I ever stopped my wife and said, "Honey, wait—where did you get that pie dish? That's beautiful. That's the most exquisite pie dish I've ever seen. Where did you get it?" I've never said that. No one has ever even thought that. Why? Because no one cares about the stupid aluminum pie dish—everyone wants the pie! The disposable pie dish is barely worth a quarter, but the pie is a rare treasure that I only get to enjoy maybe once a year.

God's message, "This light and power that now shine within us," is much better than a banana cream pie. And we are just a perishable pie dish, carrying this message to others. This is great news. This means that we don't need to worry about *us*. We don't need to worry about what people think of us—the perishable containers—we just need to present the treasure. That is why sharing our faith begins with God. Our focus needs to be on him, not on us. Who cares if you are scared of what someone will think about you—what do they think about the treasure?

Here's a simple way to begin with God: Pray and ask him to give you someone to reach out to. Just ask him, "I'm yours, Lord. Use me. Give me someone to reach out to." We know from the Great Commission that Jesus wants us to reach to others. Pray this request, and he will grant it. All ministry needs to begin with God, not us. Remember—this is his agenda, not ours.

Reach Out

Since the guy at the mailbox is most likely not going to ask us for Jesus, how can we open the door to share with him? The answer that many of us don't want to hear is, "We need to be intentional about it."

Evangelism is intentional

Allow me to clarify. Being intentional about something doesn't mean we have to become freaks. My kids need love and attention from their father. I could see this need and respond in either polar direction. I could say, "Forget the little snots! It's their mother's job to raise them!" and ignore them most of the time. Most people would agree that would probably not be a good idea. My kids would probably grow up to be pretty tweaked individuals, and I would probably become single. But let's consider the polar opposite. What if I was convicted so deeply with the realization that I needed to be with my kids that I quit my job to stay with my kids *all the time*. I would then sleep in the same room as them, follow them around, go to school with them, brush their teeth for them, cling to them—I think you get the idea.

Both of those are extreme examples of intending to spend time with my kids. Intentionality doesn't mean extreme. If you are intentional about evangelism, you don't have three friends dressed in camouflage hiding on your roof and peering through binoculars at approaching traffic.

"Charlie, this is Bravo. Come in, Charlie."

"I read you, Bravo. Over."

"Charlie, we have a red Toyota Celica, license plate 3, Victor, Bravo, 9, 4, 7, Alpha approaching. Copy?"

"Copy that, Bravo. That's my neighbor Kevin. He's an atheist. Everyone at your posts!"

"Copy that, Charlie. We've got his radio preset for KLOVE, and we have tracts hidden throughout the house."

"Did you get the VCR?"

"It's loaded with *The Jesus Film* and ready to go, sir!"

"Roger that. When he gets into the bedroom, start Operation Living Hell!"

"Copy that, Charlie. We have the thermostat rigged. Falwell's message on hell is cued and ready to be played through the system we installed in his attic! Over!"

The only thing that would be over would be your relationship with your neighbor.

Being intentional might just mean finding out what your neighbor likes. If your neighbor likes baseball, and he's always wearing a Cubs jacket—I don't care if you hate baseball—peek at the paper and find out how they're doing so you have something to talk about at the mailbox.

Don is a friend of mine who knows how to reach out to kids effectively. Don has a rare form of muscular dystrophy and never has been able to run, jump, or play sports. He relies on full leg braces to help him walk, and he even has to hold his head up with his hand because his neck muscles are so weak. He has depended on God throughout his life to get past his disability, and now he directs the campus ministries division at Youth for Christ in Sacramento. Despite his disability, Don is an expert at reaching out to others!

Years ago when Don was in San Diego, he started a campus outreach club at a local high school. Because of Don's disability, he was never able to play football. But because all Don could do was watch and learn, he became an expert at football strategy and technique. Throughout high school Don helped coach his teams, and players would count on his input. Don was a great asset to the team because he was so accurate at predicting what play the opposing team would run next.

Don put this knowledge to great use when he first visited the school he was going to reach. Don, in his wheelchair at the time, rolled up to the high school football game on a Friday night. He rolled his wheelchair right up behind the freshmen football team while they were watching the varsity game. One group of guys was particularly vocal about the game, predicting what the team would do next and what they should have done previously. Don watched for a few minutes and chose his timing wisely. While the varsity team huddled up, Don spoke up, predicting the next play. The freshmen all turned to see the 100-pound skinny guy in the wheelchair. They turned their attention back toward the field as the ball was hiked and then watched in amazement as the team ran the play that Don had predicted.

The freshmen didn't think much of it until the quiet voice from behind them spoke again, this time predicting what both teams would do. The ball was snapped, and both teams proceeded as if Don was pulling their strings and directing their moves.

This continued throughout the game, and now the freshmen were surrounding Don, asking him questions and enjoying the game with him. Finally, Don gave a prediction so skewed that even the freshmen, who had been very convinced of Don's ability, didn't believe it.

Don told them, "All right. If you think I'm wrong—back it up! I'll bet you all that I'm right. If I am, you all have to buy me a soda from the snack bar. If I'm wrong, I have to buy you all pizza after the game." The freshmen eagerly took the bet and focused all attention on the field. The varsity team ran a play far from anything that Don had (purposely) predicted. The freshmen team cheered, giving each other high fives and congratulating each other on their victory.

With his head held low, Don spoke up: "I guess I gotta take all you guys out to pizza!"

Don spent the next hours laughing, joking, learning kids' names, and having a great time. Those freshmen became the beginning of a Campus Life club that grew to hundreds of unchurched kids weekly. Those same freshmen became extremely close to Don. They would carry him across the beach in San Diego so he could hang out with them. Don developed deep relationships with those guys and eventually shared Christ with them. It all started with his intentionally reaching out to them.

We talked about some of this in our chapter on framing. But what does this actually look like? What are elements of reaching out to someone? Is it merely meeting with someone? Reaching out means listening to her, using her name, noticing what she likes.

Listening

I once met with a guy who had some equipment we were interested in renting for a huge ministry event. A coworker of mine knew the guy and introduced us over lunch. For about 12 minutes this guy never even looked at me; he just talked with my coworker. He did shake my hand when my coworker first introduced us, and he grunted something like "Yeah, yeah," before returning to his conversation. Finally, my coworker let him know that I was in charge of this big event coming up and was interested in renting some equipment. He finally looked at me, said, "Cool," and then talked for about another eight minutes without pause about how great his stuff was. Have you ever met anyone like that? Someone who ignores you for the majority of the conversation and doesn't let a peep out of you for more than 20 minutes?

In his best-seller *The Seven Habits of Highly Effective People*, Steven Covey writes, "Seek first to understand, then to be understood." (St. Francis prayed that, too!) Before we share the message that God has burdened our hearts with, we must reach out to a person by seeking first to understand him. A huge part of this is listening. People listen to those who listen. You have two ears and one mouth—use them proportionally. People like to be heard.

Names

When you first meet someone, ask him his name and don't forget it. Write it down if you have to. When talking with him, use his name several times in the conversation. This will help you remember. This doesn't mean talk like a salesman who calls during dinner: "Mr. McKee, how are you doing Mr. McKee? Mr. McKee, on behalf of Smell Gas Company, we want to offer you, Mr. McKee, a valuable service, Mr. McKee." I always want to change my name after those conversations. Just be real and do what you have to do to remember his name so you can use it genuinely.

I was running a junior high campus outreach when I met a kid named Jared. I talked to him for a while—asked about his basic interests and so on—and then I went on to meet a pile of other students. After every three or four kids I would look back and repeat the students' names to myself. A week later I was on campus again, and I saw Jared. I said, "Hi, Jared" and smiled at him. Jared almost fell over. He fumbled out a "Hi," and we began to talk. I then asked him about some of the things we had talked about the first time I met him, and he started opening up to me like we were old friends.

A name is powerful. Use it. Remember it. It will open doors you never knew existed.

Notice

Notice people's interests. If you're meeting teenagers, this is easy. They usually will wear it right on their T-shirts: their favorite bands, movies, or pastimes. This is an open door to their interests. "So, Billy, you like the band Scum Sucking Corn Muffin Stompers?" Notice what kind of car someone drives and any bumper stickers she might have. Notice what she talks about. When you find someone's hot topic, you've opened a door that sometimes you wish you could close. Regardless, noticing her interests will open a doorway to conversation with her.

An eighth-grade student rolled up on his skateboard to the door of the junior high gym where we met weekly for a campus outreach. I immediately learned his name was Tim and started asking him about skating. Now I know just enough about skating to hold a conversation with an eighth grader who rides up on a skateboard. If you notice a lot of students you work with riding skateboards, you better learn a little about skating. What is the number one desire they have? A place to skate. What is the number one complaint they have? No place to skate. Nobody wants them—they're nuisances. What is their feeling about adults and authority in general? Adults think they're nuisances and are out to get them. Knowing these facts, are you going to approach a conversation with a young man on a skateboard differently? Absolutely!

I asked Tim, "Is there any place to skate around here?"

"The schools, if we don't get chased off by the janitors."

"I bet that's frustrating."

"Yeah, they've got basketball courts for people who want to play hoops, a track for people who want to run, and stupid tennis courts for tennis players—but they're always neglecting the skaters!"

"That doesn't seem right."

Tim didn't do what he did with every other adult he came into contact with—duck his head down and walk by silently. Tim stood by me the rest of the night, talking about different skating styles and tricks and asked me questions about what we were doing there and why.

Being intentional about going where people are, listening to them, using their names, and noticing their interests will lay the groundwork to building relationships with people.

Invest Yourself

One of my friends runs a campus ministry in one of the most affluent neighborhoods in the area. Rob spends a lot of time on campus, at football games, and anywhere that kids hang out. One day last summer Rob was running some errands, and he was struck with a strong feeling that he should go by the school where he ministered. He couldn't understand why because this was the middle of the summer. He started to ignore the feeling, but his heart told him to go. He turned off toward the school and pulled into the almost empty parking lot. He saw one of the office workers struggling, trying to carry a heavy cooler from her car. Rob ran over to help her, and she thanked him again and again. After helping her Rob wondered why he was there. He thought maybe he was supposed to talk to one of the teachers he knew. He asked one of the few office workers if that teacher was here, and he was informed that she didn't work there anymore. Discouraged, Rob left the office building and started toward his car.

A small voice from across the quad yelled, "Rob...Rob!" Rob looked and saw one of the junior high girls he had worked with last year running toward him. She threw her arms around him and said, "Oh Rob, I knew you'd come—I knew you'd come! We're all graduating today." Rob, being the man of integrity that he is, did what many of us would have done at that moment: "Brianna...I wouldn't have missed it for the world."

Brianna proudly brought him into a room full of about 50 students and some faculty. Rob greeted a crowd of smiling students, gave high fives, and sat in the area where parents and family were supposed to sit. This was the graduation for all the summer school kids. Most of these kids hadn't passed one or more of their classes during the school year, but by completing summer school, they were now graduating eighth grade. Rob took his seat in the empty section. Not one parent, uncle, cousin, brother, sister, or even grandma was there. Rob cheered, clapped, and whistled as 46 kids received their junior high diplomas. Brianna came up to Rob afterward with tears in her eyes and said, "Rob, you can be my dad anytime!"

Rob came home a different person. That empty room where Rob had sat reflected a perfect picture of our society: empty kids with empty lives in an empty room. His investment in their lives—on campus or wherever they are at—opens more doors than anything else he does.

If you are in youth ministry, go where kids are—visit them on campus, see them at sporting events, and meet their families. I've worked with hundreds of youth workers in my years of youth ministry, and one of their biggest mistakes is assuming that kids will come to them. So often we think that if God wants us to reach someone, he'll drop them in our lap, attentive and ready to listen. That's not the case. The majority of the population isn't going to church anymore. Our church musical, our youth rally, and our vacation Bible school are only going to reach a small percentage of people. The rest of the people have perceptions of the church and of Christians that repel them from ever going to any church event. This leaves us no choice but to go to them.

Jenny Morgan from the Youth for Christ national office told me about a Tacoma YFC youth guidance director who became a Lutheran minister. She includes this story in YFC's national training tour, "Changing Lives Forever."

There were about a half-dozen cowboy-type kids gathered early on a Friday morning at a park just across the street from the high school in the eastern Montana town of Laurel. This same group gathered there every morning. With the shape of Copenhagen cans visible in their rear pockets, these were the kids on the edges of the local high school society—kids who could use a friend and probably haven't seen much of Jesus.

But this Friday morning was different. It was different because someone had observed this gathering of kids and had decided to put some action behind the feelings of the heart. So into this cold morning arrived a man with a pot of hot cider, some cups, and an invitation to have a drink to warm up before they made their way to class. No big deal, just a friendly gesture. Everyone joined in.

The scene repeated itself the next Friday and the next. By now the kids had discovered that the man was the new minister at the Lutheran church just a couple of blocks away. But he seemed pretty nonthreatening and friendly. And he brought the cider for what was now becoming a gathering of Friday morning "ciderheads."

On the fourth week a police car rolled up. They wanted to talk to this man, the one with the cider. They wanted identification and answers because to them, this gathering was not a good idea. They told him so, but then accepted his desire to reach out to some of these young people who could, no doubt, use an adult friend. The young people warmed up even more to this minister who, for their sake, had been hassled by the cops.

For three months, all through the winter cold, the minister and the ciderheads had been getting together. Some 20 to 25 students showed up each week. They drank cider, talked, and sometimes laughed. They had accepted this minister who wanted to be their friend. No, he wasn't pitching his church. Nor was he leading kids to Christ. But something is happening. What was happening was that Jesus was meeting with that group of kids over cider on Friday mornings. As God came in the flesh—the incarnated Christ—so Jesus comes in the flesh today, through us, if we let him.

This Lutheran minister was letting him. And whatever happens to those kids, they will always, always remember those Friday mornings with the minister and the cider and the "ciderheads." And in some small way, the doorway of the heart will be opened, at least a crack, to hear the words of Jesus and maybe to know him as Savior.

The Lutheran minister couldn't help himself. He was drawn to those kids.

With all of our programs and promotion and ministry models, let's always remember the basics just as this minister did: seeing kids in need, experiencing a broken heart, and doing something about it, the way Jesus would have done.

Investing in the lives of others is simply "hanging out" with them. I consistently ask kids about their favorite things to do. The indisputable number-one answer I get is "kicking it with my friends," which means, "hanging out with my friends." One of the best ways to build a relationship with someone is to hang out with them, doing what they like to do. Go shopping with them. Go to a sports event. Get something to eat. This hanging-out time will promote conversation where you will earn trust and draw closer to them.

Ask questions and listen to what they have to say. As your relationship with others gets deeper, so can the questions you ask. Questions are one of the most powerful tools you can use to build relationships with others. I have dedicated a whole chapter of this book to asking questions and the doors that will open.

Discover Doorways

As you get to know a person better, you will begin to find opportunities to talk about deeper issues. This, of course, takes time. When you first meet someone, you don't walk up to him and ask, "Do you ever feel lonely, like no one cares?" But after knowing someone a while, conversations will usually progress a little further than, "What's your favorite football team?"

Youth Specialties, in their Artsource gallery of clip art, has a cartoon of a guy with a huge gaping hole right in the middle of his chest. The caption reads, "Filling the Void." As I look at people in the world today, I often think of that little cartoon guy with the fat hole in his torso. People all have an emptiness or a void in their lives. They are walking around and trying to fill it. They try to fill it with relationships, drugs, sex, alcohol, money, popularity—you name it, they're trying to fill the void in their lives with it. The trouble is, only one thing fills it.

Lori Salierno is an incredible public speaker who gives talks to youth. She tells the story of a time when she shared God with a young lady. In a conversation with this student Lori explained that we all have "God-shaped holes" right in the middle of our hearts. Many people try to fill the God-shaped hole with things that don't fit. After all, only one thing fills the hole: a relationship with God. If you try to put anything else in the hole, it slips right on through.

After this teenager received Christ, she went to see her family for dinner. As the family talked about various situations they were in, this new believer boldly announced, "I think we all have a God-shaped hole, and you're all trying to put stuff in your God-shaped hole that doesn't fit!" Lori tells the humorous story of this young lady converting her friends and family by simply letting them know that nothing would fill their God-shaped holes but God. Everything else slips right on through.

Discovering doorways starts with finding a person's pain, his emptiness, the void in his life. This will give you a starting point of where Christ can meet his needs, whether emotional, physical, social, or spiritual.

We aren't going to discover these doorways by osmosis. Usually it will require our noticing them and asking questions. At this stage in our relationships with people, we should be talking about deeper issues. When an opportunity arrives, ask permission to ask deeper questions. I once worked construction with a buddy who had his philosophy of life down to a tee: *Have as much fun as possible now and be a good person—then you'll go to heaven.* We would have interesting conversations on the way to our job sites every day as he shared how hard he'd partied or who he'd slept with the previous weekend. He was currently sexually active with his girlfriend Tori, who was also sexually active before they met.

Sometimes within 10 minutes of sharing his "highlights," he would end up sharing how rotten something was going in his life. I remember once he was sharing about the past relationships he'd had and how they never worked out. I asked him if, at the time, he thought that the particular girl might have been "the one." He admitted that sometimes he thought that. I asked him if he ever regretted sleeping with any of them. He gave me various reasons why he didn't regret it. Then I did something. I asked him, "Ken, can I ask you a question?" This got his attention, and he nodded. "Do you wish Tori never slept with any other guys in the past?" This question made him think. I never would have asked him that question if we hadn't spilled our guts to each other every morning on the way to work. I had earned that right and asked him a question that made him think.

Getting permission to ask a deeper question does something else. It gets people used to our asking them permission to ask them something. That is, of course, what we are eventually going to do when we ask them if we can share something with them and share our faith. My good friend Leonard always told me, "Nothing opens the door to share your faith with someone better than a well-placed question." And he's right. Earlier in this book we talked about developing a sensitive approach. I watched God use Leonard to change lives with his sensitive approach and well-placed questions.

Leonard used to go to a park behind the school where he ministered and meet students as school let out. They all knew he would be there and they would literally line up to talk with him. Why? Because he would listen! They didn't know why, but they knew he cared about them. For most of them he was the only adult in their lives who showed any interest in them.

Leonard learned how to ask questions. He used questions that set a pace, slowly opening people up to comfortable conversation. Questions are powerful door-opening tools. The entire next chapter is devoted to door-opening questions and examples you can use.

Another doorway we can discover with someone is common struggles you face. We talked a little about this in the framing chapter. When someone shares about a loss or a specific feeling, chances are you might remember a time in your life when you felt like that, too. Use this opportunity to open a door. For example, a friend shares how upset she is because her boyfriend broke up with her. Most girls have had a breakup with a boyfriend and know the feelings that go along with a breakup. Use these to identify with an individual and understand where she is coming from. This might open the door to share how you found hope in that situation.

"Michelle, you sound like you feel empty. I remember when something similar happened to me. I was in 10th grade, and I..." (If you tell a story, be brief. What a person really wants is someone to listen, not lecture.) "...and I felt absolutely empty inside. You know the one thing that gave me hope through the whole situation? God. He always gives me hope no matter how empty I feel." Our stories are little pieces of our testimony that point to God's work in our life. We can use these little stories in appropriate places to illustrate God's love in tough situations.

My friend Bob went to a seminar on "How to Share Our Faith" taught by Phil Downer, president of CBMC ministries. Phil taught the importance of one's personal testimony when sharing our faith with someone else. Phil gave examples of five totally different testimonies. When he was done, he asked people to describe the differences between the testimonies. People responded with numerous examples, as the stories were very different. Phil then asked what the testimonies had in common. Responses varied, mostly pointing out that they all involved changed lives and a distinct turning point in which they gave their lives up to Christ.

Phil then surprised the crowd with an observation no one knew— all five testimonies were from the same person. They were all Phil's. Phil taught a very important point that day. Our lives are full of stories—stories of trying to live life on our own, without God, and failing miserably. Then something happened in our lives. We came to our senses. For some of us that was at a distinct moment, but for a lot of us that was a process. Life's consequences kept slapping us in our faces in different ways, and we slowly realized that our way wasn't working and we needed something else. So at a specific moment we gave control of our lives to Jesus. From that point on, many changes happened in our lives.

Most of us could share 20 different testimonies that are all ours. Please understand—I'm not asking you to make up a past of drugs and alcohol or a life as a satanist who came to his senses when his plane crashed, and he was the only survivor. Since our lives are full of stories of our emptiness before Christ and our fullness after Christ, pick some of those stories and use them. We can model "openness" by being vulnerable and opening up a little. This vulnerability will open more doorways to opportunities to share.

Another great doorway we can use is by inviting people to "door-opening" events. This could be as simple as inviting someone to go to church with you or as strategic as bringing her to an event of some kind where the gospel will be shared. Taking someone most likely will only be a door opener. The burden will still be on you to ask her about it. "What did you think of church?" or "When the speaker talked about Jesus being the only hope that the world offered, what did you think about that?" I've had great conversations with people after they went to church or an evangelistic crusade with me.

It's important to remember our approach when we invite someone to something like this. Church or a Christian event might be a serious step for someone. If he stretches that far, don't push him over the edge. Don't push him into a major theological discussion on the way home or put pressure on him during an invitation to respond.

One of my staff members shared her story of facing too much pressure. These friends of hers kept inviting her to church and events. She tried church a couple times and thought it was okay. Then they invited her to a Billy Graham Crusade. She shares that for her, at that time, this was a huge step. She didn't really want to hear someone preach about, in her opinion, how messed up she was and how much she needed Jesus. At the end of the event Dr. Graham gave an invitation for people to come forward and make a decision to follow Jesus. Her friends simply told her, "If you want to go down, we'll wait for you." This really made her mad. She felt like everyone was watching her, like she was something dirty that needed to be cleaned. I know the people who brought her, and they are wonderful people. And, to be honest, they didn't do anything wrong. I just think we need to remember to be careful to open doors but not stick our feet in them.

Get Permission to Share the Gospel

I introduced this BRIDGE section as how to get from "Hi, how are you?" to "Can I share something with you?" So our short-term goal up to this point has been to get to the stage where we can ask, "Can I share something with you?" Remember, we could simply walk up to someone and say, "Can

I share something with you?" But most likely we're going to have a little trouble with that because we haven't developed trust and earned the right to be heard. But here we are now: We've already *Begun with God, Reached out, Invested in their lives, and Discovered doorways.* This all might have taken us years or just a short time to accomplish. Regardless, we are ready to get permission to share the gospel with kids. How do we do this?

Once we've discovered a doorway, we simply need to ask permission to share something with them. For example, let's say you were talking about some deep issues with a friend and you got the opportunity to share your story or your testimony with her. "And I had never felt so empty in my life. I went to this church service, and the pastor shared something that changed my life—in all my years of going to church I never heard anything so simple. Can I share with you what he said?"

Most likely the person is going to say, "Yes," and you are now at the easy part: Share the gospel message!

A local youth pastor called me up and asked me if I remembered a kid named Stephan from a recent snow retreat where I had spoken. I couldn't forget Stephan. Stephan was a kid who had just started going to the youth group. He had never gone to church before, and some girls from school invited him to this youth group. He came and he loved it. He liked the fact that there were girls there, and he enjoyed the activities.

I sat with Stephan in the back of the 15-passenger van for the entire two-and-a-half-hour drive into the mountains. Stephan talked nonstop about himself: how much he loved rap music, how tough he was, how many times he had been suspended that year, the list went on. I never once rebuked him for his taste in music. I never shook my head in disapproval at his apparent behavior problem. I just listened and asked questions. I was a good listening ear, so by the time we got to the snow, I was his best friend.

All weekend when I spoke, he was in the front row, absorbing every word. Between talks, at dinner, and during free time he would hang out with me and ask me questions. I didn't have to preach at him; he came to me. He never made a decision that weekend, but he listened. Seeds were planted.

When his youth pastor called me, he asked if I could get together with Stephan. I gladly accepted. Stephan had been watching bad movies on his parents' cable TV, and he had been looking at pornographic sites on the Internet. Stephan was no different than many kids out there.

I picked up Stephan and took him to my favorite hamburger place. We ordered fries—the good potato wedge kind—and we smothered them with jalapeño cheese. After laughing and shooting the breeze for a while, I brought up the reason for being there.

"So Dave [the youth worker] tells me you've been watching some girlie flicks and doing the same on the Internet."

Stephan was embarrassed. Let's face it—who wants anyone else to know their private stuff? "Yeah, I don't know why I do it."

"I do! Women are pretty stinkin' attractive!"

Stephan looked at me surprised, then cracked a smile. "Yeah."

"It's hard to not look at that stuff when it's readily available, huh?"

"Yeah."

"You know, you're not going through anything different than any other guy is going through. You're not alone. Girls are pretty desirable—that's the way God made them. Let me ask you a question." Before I went on, I wanted his permission. He nodded. "When you go to the youth group, church, the retreats, all that stuff, what do you think of all that talk about God?"

Stephan gave the number one teenage response: "I don't know."

"Well, let me ask you a different question. Why do you think Dave has this youth group? Why do they have that church? What do you think it's all about?"

This was a deep question, and Stephan thought hard. "I don't know. They want to worship God and stuff, I guess."

"Stephan, you've been going there what—six months?"

"Yeah"

"Don't you want to know why they have a building there, why they meet? I mean, what is all this for anyway?"

"I don't know."

"Can I tell you? 'Cause I think it might answer a lot of the questions about what's going on in your life right now."

Stephan was actually pretty curious. "Sure."

I took two napkin holders, a pocket Bible, and a basket of fries and used them as illustrations as I shared the gospel with him. When I finished, he said something I never forgot. He sat back in his chair, staring at the objects I had used to illustrate the gospel, then he exhaled and looked up at me. "This is so simple! Why doesn't anybody just say it simply like this?"

I can only thank God for his help over the years, opening my eyes to how to share my faith. I used to make it so difficult. I used to cloud up the gospel message with all kinds of tangents that weren't important to the gospel message. But the gospel is a simple, life-changing message that happens to bring up the most difficult decision most people will make in their lives. Think about it. Stop doing everything you're doing, turn 180 degrees, and walk the other way, trusting in God every step. Absolutely simple message, incredibly difficult to do.

There are hundreds of ways to get permission to share the gospel. The important thing is to use the open doors we have to get permission to share.

Embrace

After someone begins a relationship with God, we need to embrace her. Not just a hug, but a whole process of letting her know she's in a new family that wants to love her, be there for her, and support her.

Affirmation and a hug are great ways to start this. If someone prays and asks God to forgive his sins and to come into his life, I always give him a hug and say, "Welcome to the family of God!" I immediately try to introduce him to other believers. I walk him up to another believer and say to the new believer, "Tell her what you just did." This is sometimes difficult or intimidating for the new believer, but it does two key things: It makes him verbalize the commitment he just made, and it gives him an opportunity to be affirmed by a fellow believer.

I once introduced a junior high kid to a relationship with Christ in a fast-food joint—just me and him. After he prayed "the prayer," I gave him a hug and a noogie and affirmed him, telling him, "That's the best decision you'll ever make in your life!" No one was around, so we went to a pay phone. I called another guy on my staff at work and said, "Here, Brian wants to talk to you." I handed the phone to Brian, the new believer, and told him to tell the staff guy what he had done. Brian fumbled his words until he finally expressed what he had just done. The other end of the phone responded with cheers and encouragement. Brian smiled big when he hung up the phone. He started to walk, assuming we were leaving. I said, "We ain't going anywhere; hold on." I put another quarter in the phone and dialed another staff guy, then another kid who had accepted Christ that year. We didn't leave until he had been *embraced* by at least three other people.

New Christians should be the VIPs of the church. They need to be embraced, loved, and nurtured like newborn babies. We'll touch more on this in chapter 11, "The Key to Follow-Up: Getting Them Plugged In."

chapter 9
Door-Opening Questions

Nothing sparks interest better than well-placed questions

In the previous chapter we looked at five tools that help us build relationships. One of the most effective of these tools is a well-placed question. Question asking is a fine art and deserves an entire chapter dedicated to it.

Years ago I ran a campus ministry at a junior high school. We were allowed on campus to hang out with kids and be "positive adult role models." Of course, during the school hours we weren't allowed to talk about God, but after school we could. Every Monday night we ran a fun program in their gym that brought anywhere from 75 to 200 students. The majority of these students could care less about God or church, but an open gym means basketball, friends, and maybe even food!

One Monday night we broke into small groups. This gives kids a chance to talk and be heard, as opposed to being lost in the large group. I divided the groups by grade and gender, which helped isolate maturity levels, and then we gave them each an opportunity that most of them had never been given before: The opportunity to be heard.

We identified a hat, called it "the conch," and placed a bucket full of questions or thought-provoking statements in the middle of the circle. We established ground rules: Only the person wearing "the conch" got to speak and no disrespecting others in any way. As the exercise went on, something magical happened. Kids started opening up doors to areas of their lives they had never shared with anyone. I'll never forget an eighth-grade girl drawing a paper out of a hat and reading, "It's okay to be raised by one parent." She started crying. "It's okay because I'm okay with it. I mean, it's not okay that my mom is addicted to crack…it's hard growing up like that. I know most of you don't understand, and that's okay…there's not much I can do about it anyways—that's just the way it is." You could hear a pin drop. Students shared feelings about love, about sex, even about God, all because they were given an opportunity to be heard by peers and a caring adult.

People want to be heard. One of the best ways to open the doors to deeper conversation is through well-placed questions. What questions can open doors to relationship building? My friend Leonard developed a list of the questions he found himself using again and again. Let's take a look at these questions, arranged by subject, and how some of them can be used. With a sensitive approach, these questions not only can help you build relationships, but many of them can also lead you to an open door to present the gospel.

Door-Opening Questions

Arranged by Topic

The following questions are great for opening the door to share your faith. I included clarifications or insight after certain ones.

(WARNING: These questions only work with a sensitive approach. If you rattle these off like a parole officer or like you have an agenda, you will only close doors.)

FAMILY

How many brothers and sisters do you have?

Are your parents together?

How old were you when they divorced?

Whom do you live with?

How often do you see the other parent? Is that okay?

These questions are particularly good for teenagers. Today these questions are actually "light" in content. Years ago it would have been a deep question to ask if someone's parents are together. Today with a divorce rate of over 50 percent, a kid is in the minority if his or her parents are together.

Who are you closest to in your family?

When is there the least amount of conflict in your home?

Does your family get along?

When you fight with _____, what is it usually about?

How is it usually resolved?

Pay close attention to the above answers. You'll get a good sense of whether or not this person is close to anyone in his family. The last question, *How is it usually resolved?* will usually be answered, "It never is." Teenagers will answer, "I go in my room and put on my headphones!"

If you could tell _____ any one thing right now, and you know
you would be heard, what would it be?

This is a powerful question that can open the door to deep feelings. It's not a probing question if it's asked after the previous examples above. I've asked this question to people many times in small group settings. Without fail, whether youth or adult, at least one person in the group will tearfully share something she's been holding deep inside. I remember one teenager sitting in a small group and acting tough in front of his friends the whole evening. When it came to this question, the young man got very quiet. His eyes teared up, and he said, "If I could say anything to my mom, and I knew she would listen…I would ask her, 'How come you never hugged me?' A hug would be nice." We were all shocked as the shell of a tough kid cracked wide open in front of our eyes. He had sensed the fulfillment of his desire to be heard, all because of a well-placed question.

PERSONAL

What do you like to do for fun?

Do you have a boyfriend/girlfriend?

How long have you been together?

When did you break up?

How are you since?

Notice the progression of these questions. Again they start light. But questions about dating relationships lead to answers about breaking up. And breaking up is a doorway to a cornucopia of emotions. Anytime you tap into a feeling of emptiness or loneliness, you've discovered an opportunity to share the answer to a kid's emptiness or her loneliness—a relationship with Jesus Christ.

Do you have a job?

Do you want a job?

Do you play sports?

Which ones?

What is your favorite team?

When you are _____ (angry, happy, sad, frustrated), what do you do?

When you are lonely, what do you do? Does it help?

Many times a person will be honest and admit that his attempts don't help make the pain, the loneliness, or the anger go away. He is looking for a solution; you only need to provide it for him.

What accomplishment are you most proud of in your life?

What is your biggest regret in life?

This second question can be taken as a probing one if it is not asked after the first one. But if asked correctly, this question can open the door to feelings of guilt. Everyone wants to be forgiven. No one wants to carry around the "junk" they've done. Any discussion about things students regret opens the door to introduce a forgiveness that will give everyone a fresh start!

What is your number-one goal in life right now?

What are you doing that will get you there?

What are you doing that will take you away from this goal?

What could you do right now to improve your life?

This next question can create an opportunity for you to share your testimony or your story of how Jesus saved you. You might be able to ask, "Can I share with you a decision I made in my life that changed my outlook on everything for the positive?"

What is the happiest you have ever been? (angriest, saddest, most at peace, most hurt)

FRIENDS

Do you have many close friends?

What is important to you in a friendship?

What kind of friend are you?

Do you mostly lead or follow your friends?
Do your friends help you make better or worse choices?

Whenever someone admits she's making bad choices in her life, she might be tired of the consequences of those choices. She might be tired of the empty feeling she gets as a result of those choices. That is an open door to share with her the best choice she can ever make. You can ask her, "Can I share with you the best choice I ever made in my life?"

Do you have a best friend?

Do you ever feel lonely when you're with your friends?

Is there a friendship you know you should have right now that you don't?

Some people will admit that they feel like there is someone or something missing in their lives. This might be an opportunity to talk about an incredibley fulfilling relationship they can have that won't ever fail them.

What is the easiest thing about making friends?

What is the hardest thing about making friends?

TEENAGERS IN GENERAL
(These questions are great for teenagers or parents of teenagers.)

What do you like about your favorite style of music?

What two emotions best describe teenagers today?

Anger and loneliness are the number one answers to this second question. Loneliness is always a billboard advertising, "I'm in desperate need of a relationship!" We can provide that for them.

What are teenagers most concerned for today?

How do you think adults feel about most teenagers?
Do you think adults and teenagers can be good friends?

If you are an adult reaching a student, this will help you understand his thought process toward you. Most teenagers have the feeling that adults don't care for them at all. Teenagers' favorite thing to do is hang out. There aren't many places today where teenagers can just hang out. This world is full of signs that say, "No Loitering," "No Skating," and "No Trespassing." Youth in malls are told they can't hang out there if they aren't shopping or with an adult guardian. Youth on the street are given evil looks by passersby. No matter where students go, they are often told to leave—by an adult.

Most adults fear teenagers. They don't understand youth, so they choose to ignore them. Besides, some of them are downright scary. My wife is used to teenagers. But if she is in the mall with our own children (who are still small), I've seen her react like most adults do. If she sees a group of tough-looking teenagers hanging out, she pulls the kids in close, ducks her head, and walks past without looking. _As long as they don't see my eyes, I'm safe!_ Most adults are guilty of this. Teenagers know this. I love to throw them off guard. If I see a crowd of teenagers, I throw a big smile on my face and say, "Hi!" or, "Wassup?" They usually look surprised. _Hey, that funny looking guy is talking to me._ Then they give me a nod back or a "Not much."

A barrier exists between adults and teenagers. If you are an adult and you want to be effective at reaching teenagers, you need to know that the barrier exists and make an effort to break it by earning their trust. Well-placed questions can move you along that road.

GOD

Do you believe in God?

What do you think he is like?

What do you think makes him _____? (mad, happy, sad, cry, laugh)

People can make a fatal mistake when asking these questions. You need to understand that when you ask these, you are going to get a lot of theologically incorrect answers. This isn't our opportunity to correct students in their ignorance.

For example, Jim and Chris are on a break at work. Jim has talked enough with Chris to comfortably ask these "God questions." Chris gives his honest opinion of what he thinks God is really like: "I think God is what each person wants him to be. For some it may be the ghost of a grandfather or a respected relative who is sent back to earth to help us along. So God really is like a spirit in many forms."

Jim leans back in his chair, crossing his arms and kicking his feet up. "Well, you're about as far off from the truth as Darwin was about evolution. Here's the way it really is, despite what *some* might think!"

What does that do? It slams the door on any attempt Jim had at sharing with Chris. Jim could have said, "You know Chris, I think you're right that different people have a lot of different opinions about God. I used to have a few different opinions about God myself. But then somebody showed me something."

"What's that?" Chris asks.

"Someone showed me something cool about God in the Bible. Can I show you?"

Jim just took the conversation from discussing different theories about God to opening the door to present the biblical theory about God—or a gospel presentation. Sharing the gospel is always our ultimate goal. We can always take a conversation about belief in God and lead it toward sharing "our belief." An important thing to notice was that Jim listened to Chris' belief first. Chris probably felt listened to and valued. Chris would probably be willing to listen to Jim now because Jim has earned the right to be heard. Hopefully this isn't the first time he's listened to Chris either.

> *Do you believe in heaven?*
>
> *Who is it for?*
> *How do you think a person gets there?*
>
> *Do you believe in hell?*
>
> *Who is it for?*
>
> *How do you think a person gets there?*
>
> *What do you think heaven is like?*
>
> *What do you think hell is like?*

Much like the "God questions," these questions give someone an opportunity to share with you her theory of life after death. We need to respect her opinion and look for a door to share our faith with her, just as we discussed in the last chapter.

Have you ever heard someone use this question—"If you got hit by a Mack truck today and stood before the gates of heaven and God asked you, 'Why should I let you in here?' what would you say?" This question can be a triple bummer! First you die a violent death, but then you have to stand before an angry God who immediately tests you with probably the hardest question you'd ever have to answer. Don't put people in that position. The previous questions, however, about heaven, hell, and how a person gets there are much better questions to get a person thinking about the inevitable conclusion of life—death! They do it in a much nicer way.

Do you go to church?

Have you ever been to one?

What do you think about church?

Here is where you'll find out what students think about church. Maybe they've been raised in churches; maybe they've never been in one. Their answers will give you insight as to where they're at with the whole "church" thing.

Most people who have visited a church even once in the last two or three years will claim that they go to that church. I have kids sign an information card when they come to our on-campus outreach we run in Sacramento, California. One of the lines on the card says "church." I always get a kick out of the responses to that line. Some of the kids write descriptions like "white church on Madison Ave." About 90 percent of the kids who do write the name of a church haven't been there in the last year. They visited for Easter or with a friend, and now they call it their church. I have some relatives who haven't been to church in three or four years. Last time I was with them, they were talking about a fire at their church. It turns out they read about it in the paper. Yet they didn't hesitate to identify it as "their" church, as if they were just there last Sunday.

Be careful. This is an area where many Christians can belittle a "non-Christian." We find out someone doesn't go to church or used to go and doesn't anymore, and we drop our heads down and give them the "naughty, naughty!" look.

These questions are simply to find out their background. Have they been exposed to a loving church? Maybe they've heard the gospel before; maybe they've even made a commitment. Or maybe they felt like they didn't belong. The answers to these questions may present great opportunities for you to share with them.

Again, be careful. They expect you to do one of two things: Tell them how bad they are for not going to church or try to sell them on going to your church. This can be a great opportunity for you to disappoint them and not do either. I love doing this. I can think of numerous times I've been talking with someone and church comes up. Immediately, when people find out I go to church or that I am a minister, they put up their defenses. Why? Because they are expecting me to tell them how bad they are for not going or to try to sell them on going to my church. They'll usually talk for a while. They'll either give me a play by play of how busy their weekends are, or they'll dictate their philosophy of life that will probably start with a sentence like, "I know you're religious and all, and I've got nothing against church, *but*... (fill in a plethora of stories and excuses in this blank)."

I always come back with something like this: "Lots of churches can put me to sleep faster than an insurance seminar. My attention span is shorter than most, so I've always had a hard time paying attention in church. But then my buddy started a church for people who don't like church. I fit right in!" I've almost never walked away from that situation without raising someone's curiosity enough to ask me more about the church.

At my church, visitors feel warm and welcome, and they almost never feel like they don't belong. So I can use that method to invite them. And I know they'll hear the gospel at my church. If your church isn't a church that you think people would feel comfortable in, then you might want to think about what there is in your area that you can bring people to.

If you could ask God any one question, what would it be?

What confuses you the most about God?

Whom do you know who reminds you most of what God would be like?

What is it about that person?

What do you think God wants people to know about _____? *(himself, others, the future)*

This group of questions is just like the other questions about God. You can use these to expand on the earlier questions or to try to find out more about their thoughts on God.

> *Do you pray?*

> *What do you pray most about?*

> *Has God ever answered one of your prayers?*

I've rarely had anyone say no to the question "Do you pray?" Most people pray or have prayed. It's funny if you think about it. Most people will pray to ask for things, but when it comes to what God has for us, we don't want to listen. Regardless, these questions not only open the door to talk about to whom they pray, but also what they pray about. This gives you a peak at their needs—needs they are willing to present to God or a god of some sort.

OTHER QUESTIONS

> *If you could go anywhere in the world, where would it be?*

> *If you could only take two people with you, who would they be and why?*

> *What do you believe is the most important part of your life?*

> *Whom do you admire most?*

> *If you were going to create a hero today, what qualities would you give him or her?*

> *Do you know anybody close to that?*

> *What part of your life would you never wish on someone?*

This last question reveals to us the most painful area in someone's life. Think how much better this question is than asking, "What makes you feel empty inside?" Once we find out "their pain," we have an opportunity to present "the solution."

What excites you about your future and why?

What concerns you about your future and why?

In the last 20 years, there has been a growing trend toward "me" and "now." *It's my life, my choice—what about my rights? I want it now, charge it, buy now pay later, who cares, I probably won't live to see that age anyway!* Most people live for today. Personal debt has risen nationally. People aren't saving, aren't planning ahead, and aren't committing. Cars are leased, not owned. Marriages are shorter and families in general don't care enough about each other to invest time with each other. This world doesn't want to think about the future because they haven't paid their dues. When we talk about the future, people become terrified because they don't like what's in store for them. Consequently, people have a host of excuses and philosophies ready for the grabbing to make them feel good temporarily till the cow pie hits the fan.

God gives us something the world doesn't—*hope*. People like to be given hope. The key is finding out when to present it to them.

chapter 10

Focus on Christ (It's More Than a Tract)

Sharing Jesus' story simply, clearly, and memorably

So you've invested in someone's life, the door is open, and you have the chance to share Christ. What do you say?

I remember a time when I royally messed up a chance to share about my relationship with God. A friend and I were in sales together. We were in the car on an hour-long drive. He knew my beliefs and had asked me questions every once in a while, usually about church or why he couldn't sleep with his girlfriend. This particular day he just asked me, "So what is it you actually believe about God?"

Let's face it—this cut down to the nitty-gritty. All I had to do was clearly explain to this guy the gospel message. Here's where we need to ask, "Is a canned presentation adequate in these types of situations?"

Well, I didn't have a canned presentation. As a matter of fact, I panicked and didn't know what direction to go, so I started rambling about how the Bible was accurate and archeology supported creationism. Within two minutes I created more questions in his mind than he had when he approached me. Again I had proved to myself that I desperately needed to be able to explain to someone what God has done for me.

Most of us who have been saved by grace and have put our trust in Christ know the details of what happened. And regardless of our background, the same thing happened in each one of us. God wants a relationship with us, but each of us tried to live life *our way* instead of *his way*. This separated us from our relationship with him. We came to a point where we knew we couldn't go any farther, and we needed a savior. We became aware of the fact that Jesus paid the price for everything we have ever done wrong, and *only he* can save us from separation from God. We asked him to forgive our sins and take over our life. Now we live our life by daily putting our trust in him.

That is every Christian's testimony. We can't do it our way, so we decided to live his way. That's our story.

Have you ever shared your story?

Our Story

By now we've already learned our friend's story—maybe this is a good time to share our story. That's right—articulate exactly what Christ has done in your life. This might start when someone shares with you a little about his life. When someone shares his story, he probably will convey certain emotions.

"When my girlfriend broke up with me, I felt lonely."

"When my dad left, I felt rejected…responsible."

"When I got home from the party, I felt empty, like I was missing something."

When people share the emotions they felt, it provides a springboard for us to share a time when we felt like that. Even if we can't relate exactly to their situation, maybe we can relate to the emotion.

"I remember once when my girlfriend broke up with me. I have never felt so alone. I was empty. I wanted something to fill the loss."

"I remember once when I felt totally rejected. I figured it was all me."

"I remember thinking that I would find happiness in popularity, money, and things. Funny thing—whenever I achieved any of those things, I still felt empty."

Even if they don't share their emotions, sometimes they are implied. Even if we didn't party, we might relate to being empty inside. This opens the door for us to share our story.

Our story should always contain three elements:

1. The way it was

2. The change

3. The way it is now

"The way it was" is simply our story before Jesus. When sharing our story, we should always share how we felt before giving Jesus control of our life. This is where we can relate to or identify with some of the emotions they shared with us.

Some of us don't remember life without Jesus. Maybe we prayed to accept Jesus when we were five years old. Well, most likely we know what it is like to struggle, to try things our own way and not trust in him. When we do that, we experience loneliness, emptiness, and strife—the same emotions everyone feels at some point in their lives. If they share these feelings, we can relate to them and share how we depended on God to get through them.

The second element our story needs to contain is what I call "the change." This is what Jesus did to change our life. This is our conversion. This is the point when I realized it was time to stop doing it my way and to start doing it his way.

When we share our story, we want to clearly communicate how we felt before and how that brought us to need Jesus. Again, this might not be when we first committed our lives to Jesus, but another time when we realized we needed to trust him to fill our emptiness, mend our wounds, and fill us with joy.

The third element our story needs to contain is "the way it is now." This is what our life looks like after we put our trust in him.

"I felt alone, but now that I have Jesus, I always have someone there for me."

"I was empty, but now that I have Jesus, I am filled."

"I felt rejected, but now that I have Jesus, I feel loved."

Share what Jesus has done for you. When we share what Jesus did for us, we will show others a picture of what Jesus can do for them.

His Story

Our story can give a snapshot of what God did in our lives. But that's not the whole picture. It finally gets down to sharing his story. It finally gets down to sharing the gospel and talking about Jesus.

When my friend asked me, "So what is it you actually believe about God?" I didn't have an answer, and I left him hanging. There are tons of different methods for explaining the gospel, from the Romans Road to the BRIDGE method. Having a basic understanding of one of these methods might be a good way to prepare yourself so you won't sit there stammering like I did.

But more than having a specific method, we need to make sure the person we're sharing with understands God. Granted, we'll never completely understand God, but there are so many misconceptions about God that it's hard for an unchurched teenager to get beyond them.

Some of you may remember a commercial that started like a scene out of the movie *Armageddon*. Huge fireballs plummet to the earth, destroying buildings, landscapes, and wildlife. The scene shifts to heaven where God is pouring hot sauce on something and missing the bowl entirely. As the scene shifts back to earth, we realize that these fireballs or comets are God's drops of hot sauce that he's carelessly sprinkling on his sandwich, missing the sandwich entirely, and hitting the earth.

Just like most commercials or movies that portray God, this commercial portrayed him with a long white beard and a flowing white robe. This commercial proposed that God makes stupid mistakes. Other representations of God commonly portray him as judgmental, mean, spiteful, and definitely not fun to be around.

So many of the unchurched have a common misperception of God. They either think of God as this old, uncaring guy with the beard and the robe or as some far-out intangible being who is impersonal and unreachable.

When presenting the gospel and communicating that God loves us and wants a relationship with us, we need to recognize that these misconceptions exist. Most people today don't know that God wants a relationship with us. They don't know that he wants us to call him Daddy. They don't know that he is willing to forget our entire past if we just come home to him.

Everett's Story

Everett had a great relationship with his father growing up. His father loved him deeply and always told him so. Everett and his older brother would always play together with their father. Everett particularly liked baseball. As Everett grew up, one of his favorite times was playing catch with his father. They would laugh and talk, and Everett's dad would always affirm him in everything he did. This was weird to Everett's little friends because their dads weren't like this. You see, Everett lived in an extremely wealthy area of Santa Barbara. Most of Everett's friends were also wealthy. Their fathers unfortunately worked late hours and traveled for weeks at a time. Their fathers didn't play with them often, and the words they exchanged when they were home weren't always positive.

As Everett grew up, he began to play baseball at school. As games and practices took more and more of Everett's time, Everett's dad saw less and less of him. But at every single game, Everett could look into the bleachers just above the first-base line, and his dad was there, cheering the loudest and smiling the biggest. Here and there on a Saturday, Everett and his father would play catch or go to breakfast together, but those times started fading as Everett spent more and more time with his friends.

At first Everett's time with his friends was innocent, usually playing baseball or just plain "goofing around." But as Everett got into high school, his closer friends went to parties on Friday and Saturday nights. Everett would go, but he wouldn't drink or do anything stupid. He just liked hanging out with his friends. Everett's dad would often grab his mitt and ask, "Do you want to play catch?"

"No thanks, Dad, I gotta go to Michael's house."

Something happened. The more Everett went to parties on Friday and Saturday nights, the more Everett would want to sleep in late on Saturday and Sunday mornings. Sunday had always been the day that he and his father would spend together. Everett was often sleeping past noon on Sundays and then running out to go hang with his friends.

Everett's father finally mentioned something to him. "Everett, you know I love you, and I want the best for you…but I'm worried. You're getting in at 2 and 3 a.m. I can't have that in this house. You know I have a midnight curfew for you, for your protection."

"Dad, Michael's dad lets him stay out as late as he wants"

"That's not the point."

"That's entirely the point. You have too many rules."

"Everett, I love you. I don't want you doing something that will hurt you."

"I can take care of myself!"

Everett's father paused and looked down. "Everett, what about our time on Sundays? I miss that time. Last week I had Dodger tickets and you didn't even want to go to the game with me. What's wrong?"

"Nothing's wrong. I just want to live my own life."

"Everett, you know I'm here for you. I can help you if you're getting into trouble."

"I'm not getting in trouble, Dad. Just back off, okay?" Everett was lying. He was a senior now, and he was starting to do things with his friends that he knew he shouldn't do. He got good at hiding these things from his father. He got good at hiding these things from himself.

When Everett graduated from high school, he had already decided the path for his life. He decided he didn't want to do the college thing like his brother had done. Everett wanted to go live with his friends on the beach. After sleeping in till 1:30 in the afternoon the Saturday after his big graduation party he told his dad, "I know you're not gonna like it, and I don't want a lecture, but I'm not going to college."

His father was silent.

"I know you probably want me to be more like my brother…"

"Everett, I never wanted you to be anything—"

"Dad! Save it! I'm taking the money in the account you set up for me and going to live with Michael and the other guys. Don't try to stop me."

Everett had prepared himself for a fight, for yelling and screaming. There wasn't any. Everett was in no hurry to stay, so he grabbed his bags and left. As the door slammed, Everett heard his father begin to weep.

Everett got a condo on the beach a little bit north of his home, out by the city college. If you went to that school, you knew who Everett was because every Friday and Saturday night the biggest parties were there.

Everett's bank account wasn't small. He had the right clothes, the right cars, the right place, and the wrong friends. Everett partied for years. He didn't go to school, didn't get a job—just partied.

One day, years later, Everett was in Macy's buying a leather jacket. He tossed the cashier his credit card and tapped his fingers impatiently, waiting for the cashier who was taking entirely too long.

Finally, the cashier spoke up "I'm sorry but your card won't go through."

"That's impossible!"

"I tried it two times. Do you have another one?"

Everett tried card after card and got the same response. Finally he left the jacket with the flustered cashier and walked outside, turning on his cell phone and speed-dialing his accountant. His calls wouldn't go through, so he drove across the parking lot to a pay phone.

"Jake! What's up? I'm trying to buy a jacket and none of my cards are going through!"

"Everett, I've been trying to reach you, but your cell service is off!"

"What's up with that? What do I pay you for?"

"That's the point, Everett—you haven't paid me in three months. I've been trying to tell you to stop spending—you're broke!"

"Well, transfer some stocks into the money market."

"That's what I've been doing for months. Everett! Listen to me! There's nothing left!"

Two weeks later Everett's condo had a white piece of paper on the door—he had 30 days to get out. By now his friends were long gone—they left when the money left and Everett started selling things.

Months later Everett was walking down the street with everything he owned in a small backpack. With no car, no place to live, and no friends, Everett made his way down Highway 101 with his thumb out.

He got a ride down to Carpenteria where he was let off near some avocado farms. Everett didn't know where he was or where he was going for that matter. He saw a farmhouse off in the distance, and he thought it was worth a try. He walked up a long driveway leading to a small stucco house with a big front porch and one of those wooden porch swings. Everett rang the doorbell and stood there waiting. Everett felt worse than he'd ever felt in his entire life. He had left his family, squandered his money, wasted his life, and now he had to resort to asking for help. Ringing the doorbell was an admission of this fact.

Finally, the door was opened by a large man wearing a flannel shirt and jeans that were unbuttoned in the front. He stared at Everett from head to toe and finally barked, "Can I help you with something?"

"I don't know," Everett said, confused by what he was even doing there. "I guess I wondered if you had a place to stay or knew of a place I could stay—and work of course."

"Well ain't this a kick in the pants. I just let somebody go on Monday. You ever picked avocados?"

Everett lied. "Yeah...a little bit." He knew just how to choose them at the Vons market down the street from his place. He also made a mean guacamole dip.

"Follow me." The man took him around the house to a barn-like building in the back. There were a few animals back there and an old Mitsubishi 4x4 that had seen better days. They hopped in the 4x4, and Everett was given a tour of the place. The man showed him a place in the loft where Everett could stay. Before he knew it, Everett was picking avocados by day and shoveling horse and pig manure at night.

The job was fine for a couple of weeks. Everett had never worked with his hands, but he had always kept in good shape for baseball. He learned how to pick avocados soon enough to cover his bluff, and anyone could feed and clean up after horses and pigs.

One day in particular Everett was sitting on a fence, watching the pigs eat the leftovers of the farmer's dinner. As Everett stared down at the corn bread, he found himself getting hungry. The thought crossed his mind to grab that piece of cornbread out of the pigs' trough, but as soon as the thought entered his mind, he got mad.

I can't believe that I'm sitting here feeding pigs, thinking about eating their food. Everett looked at his hands. *Look at my hands. They're all cut and callused. And I sleep in a barn! Heck, my father's servants eat better and live in the guest house.* Everett came to his senses. *What am I doing here?*

Everett grabbed his small backpack and, without saying good-bye, left down the long driveway. He made his way to the main road, stuck his thumb out, and started heading toward home. He didn't know if his father was still there, or even if he'd take him back, but he figured it was worth a try.

After a mile down the 101 a semi picked him up. Everett rehearsed what he would say to his father when he saw him, "Dad, I know I turned my back on you. But I want you to take me back…"

He knew that wasn't the right approach. "Dad, I know I turned my back on you and you probably don't want me as your son. But maybe you would accept me as your slave or your servant…"

The truck slowed down and let him out by the old Vons shopping center. He walked up the hill, noticing his tattered clothes and the holes in his shoes. This was the first time in his life he was not dressed in the best of clothes.

Thunder clapped after a flash of light illuminated the dark redwoods reaching up to the sky. Within a minute, rain began its rhythmic banter on the curvy road. Everett pulled his torn jacket up over his head and rounded the corner into his cul-de-sac.

Everett was having second thoughts. Now that he was just a few houses away from his old home, regret and fear began to overwhelm him. But the curiosity of the moment kept his feet moving forward. After all, he didn't even know if his father still lived here.

As he approached the old house, Everett noticed how different it looked. The trees were much taller, and the outside of the house was a different color. Everett stopped and stared for a moment, then caught sight of the mailbox out by edge of the driveway. Glancing around, he slowly approached the mailbox and opened it up. A few pieces of mail were tucked safely in the dry inside of the box. Everett pulled the top letter out with his callused hand, reading the name of the recipient.

Everett didn't know whether to sigh in relief or to turn around and run away. Years of seeking fulfillment on his own had led him nowhere. His father had been right. Everett was wrong. And here he was, back at his father's doorstep, broke, dirty, shameful—a failure.

The name on the envelope was his father's. There was no avoiding it—this was his father's house. But as Everett slipped the letter back in the mailbox, he knew that he didn't have the courage to knock on the door and face ultimate humiliation.

Everett's finger brushed against something sticky on the lid of the mailbox. An old piece of paper was taped to the lid and held by an old piece of masking tape. On the tape was a smear of ink that had faded from years of weathering. Everett peered closely at the smudge of ink, trying to make out the faded word. Everett swallowed when he saw it: "Everett."

He grabbed the tape, which pulled easily from the lid of the box. The old piece of paper was folded into small squares and almost fell apart as Everett opened it. It was a letter from his father.

Dear Everett,

Welcome home, my son. There is food in the refrigerator. There are blankets in the closet. I kept your room for you just the way you left it.

The key is hidden where it always was.

Welcome home, son.

I love you,
Dad

The rain dripping from Everett's hair camouflaged the tears streaming from his eyes. He slammed the mailbox shut and started to throw the note to the ground—but he couldn't bear to part from it. So he shoved the note in his pocket and turned toward the main road.

The sky had darkened now, so Everett was able to see the headlights coming from the main road. Everett ducked behind the neighbor's front bushes. He was sure that his present appearance wasn't a welcome one, and he didn't feel like answering questions.

A car Everett didn't recognize pulled into the driveway of his old house. Everett kept his head low, peering through the wet leaves of the neighbor's shrubs.

A man stepped out of the car, gathered his things, and shut the car door. He started to head into the house but stopped and turned toward the mailbox.

Everett stayed low and strained to see the face of the man's silhouette against the pink and purple sky.

The man approached the mailbox and opened the door, pulling out the mail. As the man turned to face the box, Everett recognized his face.

His father had aged quite a bit. His gray hair was thin and combed neatly back behind his ears. His kind eyes scanned the mail quickly, not satisfied with what they saw. But then his father froze for a few seconds that seemed like an eternity to Everett. His father rubbed his thumb against the empty spot on the mailbox lid, finally shutting the lid and scanning the street for a sign of movement. His eyebrows were raised and his eyes full of hope.

He tucked his mail with his other papers and moved quickly for the front door. Everett stayed low, his legs cramping from squatting so long. His feet were in topsoil, and there was no place to sit.

As his father disappeared into the house, Everett started to get up from his cramped position. As Everett took a few steps out into the open, the houselights from his old house came on, and the big driveway light lit up the street. Everett didn't move as he saw his dad go to the front window and peer outside.

Everett was in plain view. He didn't move. He figured his father wouldn't recognize him. But his father stared intently through the window. Across the street and through the rain, Everett stared into the eyes of the old man behind the large pane of glass. The kind eyes saw beyond the dirt and wear on Everett's face, and they lit up with excitement.

Before Everett could move, his father ran to the front door, flung it open, and ran through the rain toward Everett.

Everett didn't know what to do. He stood there for a second before remembering the speech he'd rehearsed.

But it was more that he could bear. His father was running beyond the ability of a man that age. His arms were outstretched, and his eyes were flooded with tears. As his father caught him, Everett fell into his arms. Tears burst from his eyes, and he couldn't hold back the sobs of anguish. Cradled in his father's arms, Everett enjoyed a feeling he hadn't felt in years—a hug from his daddy.

His father bellowed, "Everett, my son. You've come home! Welcome home, my son!"

Everett tried to get out the words he'd rehearsed, but his father wouldn't have any of it. He grabbed Everett's head and buried it in his chest and held him tighter than Everett had ever been held before.

"I don't care where you've been. I don't care what you've done. I'm just glad you're home. Welcome home, my son."

Overcome the Misconceptions

This story is just a rip-off of the powerful story of the Prodigal Son that Jesus tells in Luke 15. The important part is this point: God doesn't care about your past, he doesn't care what you've done, he's got his arms open wide, and he wants you to come home.

We need to explain God's story in a way that overcomes the misconceptions people have. Sometimes that will require going beyond the Four Spiritual Laws with a story like the one above. That story pushes people far beyond the idea that God is some uncaring, detached geezer up in the clouds.

Jesus Is the Only Way

Many unchurched teenagers have a hard time grasping the concept that Jesus is the only way to God (remember chapter 3?). If that's the case with the student you're talking to, be prepared to help her understand why

Jesus is the only way. I always like to read John 14:6 to people when I'm talking about Jesus: "Jesus answered, 'I am the way and the truth and the life. No one comes to the Father except through me.'" That concept is all throughout the Bible (John 1:12; John 3:16; Romans 6:23; Romans 10:9; 1 John 5:11-12), but don't just club her with Scripture.

Whatever misconceptions you face, approach them with grace and tenderness. This isn't a debate—it's a conversation. Some preconceived notions are harder to deal with than others. Think about how much time Jesus spent dealing with messed up ideas about God. And the student you're talking with might not get it the first time. That's okay. It might take a while—and that's when we go back to youth ministry in one word: *love*. He's heard the story, and now he'll continue to see you living it.

Praying for Salvation

If a student does decide she wants a personal relationship with Jesus, that's awesome! Pray with her right then and there. I always like to have students pray in their own words. I've seen teenagers make a decision for Christ and pray with someone, then five minutes later I asked what they prayed, and they couldn't even verbalize it. If they can't verbalize it, how can they live it?

If a student says he wants a relationship with God, have him articulate what he wants. Make sure he understands what he wants to do.

Then it's time to pray. I tell the student I'll pray first, then she will. I'll review the basics of the gospel and what one needs to do. As I pray first, I'll thank God for the student sitting with me and for the fact that she's going to accept Christ. This is a good chance to summarize again what she should pray. Then let her say it in her own words. If she needs help or can't remember the words, be patient and help her out.

Amen!

Now What?

Good question. Glad you asked. And I wrote a whole chapter to answer that question.

chapter 11

The Key to Follow-Up

Getting them plugged in

The focus of this book has been reaching out to the unchurched. You reach out to them, you serve them, you care for them, you befriend them, and hopefully they meet Christ. So what then?

Jesus asked us to make disciples, not decisions. Just because we had the privilege of introducing someone to Christ doesn't mean we become a flake from then on! How can we make sure we are making disciples of Jesus? The key is a thing we call "follow-up."

Follow-up refers to the discipleship process in a student's life after he makes a decision for Christ. As youth workers we should be making a long-term commitment to a life, not just a short-term sales pitch.

Most students value relationships. No one wants to be our project, but they do want to be our friends. The last few years brought us several movies with this theme: *10 Things I Hate About You, She's All That,* and *Never Been Kissed.* All of these films contain someone who finally discovers he or she was just a project, a bet, or an assignment. Not a pleasant discovery!

I remember a student named Jesse who I met through our on-campus ministry. Jesse and I ended up spending quite a bit of time together. We grabbed fast-food together, I gave him rides when he needed them, and we hung out together at our Wednesday-night outreach. A week didn't pass when Jesse wasn't with me going somewhere.

As Jesse and I got closer, I had the chance to share the gospel with him. Jesse gave his life to Christ and started attending church. That's when I dumped him. I never called him again!

(No, that's not what I did. But can you imagine? He accepts Christ and, "Mission accomplished—I'm through wit' you!")

No one would want that kind of ending, but I've seen it happen. If our passion is evangelism, we might have a tendency to move on to someone else who needs Christ. But what does this tell the person we've befriended? It tells her she was merely a project, and now she's been checked off our list.

When we help someone become a new Christian, we need to understand the responsibility it entails to love and equip the new believer. Evangelism includes *responsible newborn care*. New Christians should be the VIPs of the church because, however you plan to follow-up, you can be sure Satan believes in immediate follow-up.

When Follow-Up Begins

Jesse was one of the first students I led to Christ. When he gave his life to Christ, I remember thinking to myself, "What now?"

As we start our ministry, we need to begin with the end in mind. We need to think about what our end goal is for this student. Do we want him to just hear the gospel? Or would we like to see his life changed? Most of us would like to see him plugged into a church. So for those of us involved in parachurch ministries we need to try to involve the church in the process in its early stages. Sometimes ministries don't do this, and then church comes as a culture shock.

I faced this difficulty early in my ministry with Youth for Christ. Our ministry was a campus ministry, so most of our students didn't attend church. Even though our outreach meetings always led to discussions about God, the students weren't used to some of the typical ingredients of a church: worship, time in prayer, and deep studies in God's Word. Even though our ministry opened great doors to discussions about God, it fell short in giving a full understanding of the call to commitment that the Bible talks about.

I began to witness this when I saw students come to Christ. They wanted a relationship with God and were excited about their faith—but then the first Sunday came around. "I gotta get up at what time?" And "I can't do what on Saturday night?"

I found that even though I had a large number of decisions to follow Christ, I had a small number of commitments to Christ. Regardless of our denomination or our theological belief, we all want to see people committed to him. We'd all like to see people who put their faith in Jesus take steps toward getting to know him better, let the Holy Spirit change them, and plug in with other believers.

Follow-up doesn't begin once someone becomes a believer. It needs to start early in the process. We need to begin with the end in mind. How do we do this?

Beginning with the End in Mind

Do you have people involved in your ministry who want to disciple students? Are they involved in your ministry right now? Do students know who they are? You might want to involve these people in the ministry in some way so the handoff to discipleship isn't culture shock.

Are the youth you're trying to reach being exposed to the church? Not necessarily the brick building down the road, but the *people* of the church?

In my campus ministry, I started involving the church earlier in the process. I worked with a local youth pastor who started attending my outreach ministry on Wednesday nights as one of my volunteer staff. This youth pastor met tons of students, and we constantly pumped church activities at our outreach events. Before we knew it, there was a bridge built that was much easier for students to cross. Students who early in the year had said, "I don't do church!" now were going to youth group on Thursday nights with this youth pastor they knew through our campus ministry.

I also began shuttling kids to church. Our ministry bought a 15-passenger van that we filled with kids each week and we took them to church. Students who were just "seeking" or just "checking things out" got used to going to church on Sundays. Some got plugged into small groups and attended Bible studies.

I see churches doing the same thing. They begin their ministry with the end goal in mind. A local youth group in my hometown has campus-based outreach meetings in homes around town. These groups attract students from specific school campuses in the area. Although these particular meetings are very focused on outreach, their goal is to spark an interest in Christ and plug unchurched students into the youth group. The group has a Sunday-morning youth service, weekend activities, small group Bible studies, and student leadership programs. Students who attend the outreach meetings hear about all the fun stuff going on the rest of the week and naturally start to plug in. By the time students make a decision for Christ, most of them are already plugged into the church.

Immediate Follow-Up Musts

There are three essentials we must not omit when someone comes to Christ through our ministry.

1. Make sure new Christians are contacted quickly.

I mentioned earlier that Satan believes in immediate follow-up. I've seen this firsthand in my ministry. In the first two years of my ministry I witnessed huge conflicts, crisis, or opposition within the first day or two of students coming to Christ. Students would get in fights with their parents—who weren't Christians—and end up grounded from all church activities. An old habit or temptation would surface and make a student feel guilty, and she would withdraw.

Now I'm not one of those people who have *This Present Darkness* sitting out on my coffee table instead of the Bible. But after seeing this time and time again, I decided to try to get a jump on ol' Satan. Whenever I led a student to Christ, I let him know he'd probably be tested in the next couple of days. I warned him that Satan would do something to make him feel like his commitment was a joke. Then I promised I would call him a day or two later and ask him what test he faced.

This worked. Students would call me even before I had a chance to call them. They told me about some temptation or some freak occurrence that happened and how they claimed victory over it.

Immediate follow-up is necessary. A call within the first few days is a great way to do that.

2. Give them a Bible.

Would you go into battle without a sword? Would you enter a fast-food kiddie playground without a can of disinfectant? No. Then don't let a new believer enter the world without a Bible.

And how about a Bible she can read and understand? There are some great student Bibles out there with all kinds of extra devotionals and notes that explain tough passages. Have a box of these Bibles handy so you can get them in the hands of new believers when they come to Christ.

I used to keep a pocket New Testament with me at all times, and I can't tell you how many times I ended up giving it away. Then I'd go home and reload my pocket from my box of 100 pocket Bibles (that I paid less than $2 apiece for!).

Don't just give students Bibles—mark a page where they should start reading. When I worked with unchurched junior high students, I always told them to start in the book of Mark. Opinions will vary, but I felt like it was a great start for junior high kids.

In short, get them in the Word right away!

3. Ask permission to go through follow-up material with them.

The last thing I like to do when I lead someone to Christ is set up a time to meet with her again so we can go through a book together.

In my years of ministry, I always told new believers a story that my friend Leonard told me. I told them that my friend said the best day of his life was his wedding day. His wife looked beautiful, he was all spiffed in a tux, and all of their friends were there. So they walked down the aisle, said their vows, and kissed. Then they each went out a separate door and never saw each other again.

I always love to see the look on a kid's face when I say that. But then I go on.

No, that is not what happened. They left together and lived in the same house.

When you have a relationship with God, you live in the same house. It's a commitment to a lifelong relationship. And unlike many marriages today, this commitment is forever.

I always tell students that if they want to get to know God better, they should spend some time getting to know him. Then I tell them I'd like to help them do that. I ask if they'd like to go through a book with me.

There are many great discipleship guides available. I give one away for free on our ministry's Web site because discipleship is essential.

When a new believer begins a relationship with God, set up a time to start going through a follow-up book with him.

More Follow-Up Musts

We could write an entire book about follow-up. But here are some quick principles to consider as you plan your follow-up with new believers:

* Assure them of their salvation. Make sure new believers understand the nature of what has happened in making a decision to follow Christ. Provide biblical assurance that will guide them in the first few weeks with Christ.

* The relationship is more important than the material. Don't get mad at them if they "flake" on you or if their interest in God seems to fade. We need to love them regardless. We need them to understand that our love is unconditional.

* Be interested in more than their relationship with God. Once they accept Christ, don't meet with them for Bible studies only. If you used to hang out for fun, continue to hang out for fun, too. Don't make them feel like your relationship got boring once they accepted Christ.

* Match the material to the kid. Choose your discipleship material carefully. Don't take a kid that has trouble reading through a reading-intensive book.

* Begin and end in prayer. After your time together, have students end in prayer. Ask them what they learned that day, then have them thank God for that lesson.

* Set up the next meeting time and place before you leave. Sometimes it's easier to set a time when you're face to face than try to track them down and get a time.

* Don't be a stranger between lessons. Like I said earlier, your relationship should not just be about digging through a book. You've invested time into a relationship. Continue to invest in them, have fun with them, talk with them, listen to them, and develop them into followers of Christ.

Follow-up is basically about continuing everything you've been doing. The unchurched teenager you've befriended and shared the gospel with may be a Christian now, but he's still clueless about the church. Give him the same love and understanding you did before he accepted Christ.

Outreach in Action: What It Looks Like

Diverse methods for
diverse groups

You've just read an entire book about reaching the unchurched. But is anybody actually doing it?

Glad you asked. Let's look at some examples of normal people like you and me who are reaching out to the unchurched—people reaching people, students reaching students, and ministries reaching youth.

The Snowblower

I was at a seminar with a bunch of incredible speakers from around the country. As we were brainstorming about evangelism, we all started asking each other about personal evangelism. "When is the last time you led someone to Christ?" "What do you do to reach the guy next door?" As the questions got more personal, we started getting more uncomfortable. Many of us gave a story of a time we tried to talk to a neighbor. I told how my wife and I made cookies for our new neighbors when they moved in, but I hadn't talked to them since. One guy shared how he thought of having some neighbors over for dessert to just share what he believes.

As we talked about this, something happened. Here we were, most of us professional speakers or evangelists, and none of us could even shed any light on how to reach the guy next door. We all sat there kind of awkwardly, staring at our shoes and twiddling our thumbs. Finally, Rich Van Pelt, a dynamic guy who works for Compassion International, spoke up.

"I bought a snowblower."

We all looked at him like he was nuts. We're talking about evangelism here, Rich! Get on the same page! Rich lived in Denver. Of course he had a snowblower—either that or you shovel till your arms fall off!

He continued, "I finished blowing my driveway one day, and I looked at my neighbor's driveway. It was covered with snow. I had a funny feeling I should do it for her, so I did. Then I did another neighbor's. Then another's. Before I knew it, I'd cleared all the driveways on the whole street. Now I set my alarm two hours earlier if it snows. I get up, do my driveway, then all my neighbors' driveways. I don't leave a gospel tract on the door. I don't have any conditions. I just clear their driveways."

"Every time it snows?"

He smiled really big. "Every time it snows!"

I couldn't help it. I asked him, "How many houses?"

"Nine!"

The rest of us exchanged glances, smiling and nodding in approval, yet amazed by this act of service.

He laughed. "You guys—I get Christmas presents now from all my neighbors. I talk with them all when we see each other outside. When I go away to speak and they see me come back, they come over and say, 'Rich, we missed you!' I just tell them, 'It must have snowed!'" He laughed.

He got really serious. "There's a lady on one side of my house whose husband died a few years ago. The gossip around the neighborhood is that he was an alcoholic, and now she's hit the bottle. The neighbor on the other side of my house is living an alternative lifestyle! I've always tried to talk with these ladies, and I never could. But now that I snow-blow their driveways, they can't stop talking to me!"

Rich opened more doors to reach his street than anyone I know has ever opened with their neighbors. Not by dropping tracts. Not by asking if they'll listen to a presentation. But by meeting a physical need! He just uses his snowblower on their driveways.

The Breakfast Program

A coworker of mine knew of a small elementary school in a poor area of Kentucky that had a breakfast and lunch program that fed most of the children. Lunch programs were common, but this breakfast program was a great service. Kids would come to school early and get muffins and juice or milk. Poor families in the area counted on this program because it provided two free meals a day for all their children, five days a week.

State budgets changed, and the funding was cut for the breakfast portion of the program. A neighborhood church that sat right across the street from the school had a quick meeting. A team of ladies committed to volunteering their time, and some others put a budget together. The church contacted the school and told them that they would continue the breakfast program—no strings attached. The school gladly accepted.

Children would now come to the church before school and get fruit, a muffin, and some juice or milk. The church didn't require children to listen to any message; they could just get breakfast and walk across the street to school. Local families started taking an interest in this church that cared about their community and their children. Attendance in the church shot way up—because of breakfast.

The Rock (A ministry to teenagers through a church in central California)

I spoke at a camp for a church youth ministry that goes by the name Full Throttle. This ministry is unique for many reasons, one being their location. They meet off campus in a strip mall in an old liquor store. They bought out the liquor store and filled it with couches, an espresso bar, pool tables, and a great sound system. This teenage center is called The Rock. And it fills with hundreds of kids each week.

The Rock isn't just open after school; it also has weekly programs. Tuesday nights are focused on outreach and attract many unchurched kids. One of the youth leaders is the coach of the local school football team, so that helps them get to know kids on campus. Word of mouth is also huge for The Rock. People feel comfortable there, have a great time, and are ministered to. When people experience it, they want to bring their friends.

The leaders call their Tuesday-night programming method a funnel effect: Start off broad with a lot of socializing and having fun. Bring it together with a funny video that they make during the week. No games, just up-front activities with students on stage. "We found that we had a better chance of having fun with the kids just from the video and from interacting with them on stage, kind of like a Letterman style."

Then they worship and pray. "By the time prayer and worship begin, the laughing is out of our system, and everyone is ready to do business with God through worship and through the Word."

"We minister in a major metropolitan area where there are a million things to do and kids have money. That translates into unchurched kids having a lot of options on any given night. We have to answer the question that this kid has: 'Why would I come to The Rock?' Why would he leave his entertainment center, his bong, his 2001 Mustang, and his naked fatherless girlfriend to come? I believe that kid wants to laugh hard at life and at himself. He wants to cry, he wants his questions that he never asks anybody answered, and he wants to know there is a God."

They take preparations seriously. "If we can't bring kids into the presence of God during worship, or if we make his Word boring due to lack of preparation, then we aren't doing our job as pastors."

Disruption isn't tolerated at The Rock. "Our kids know that's when it's time to do business with God. If you disrupt worship or time in the Word, you're going home. We have to provide an environment where it's safe for anyone to worship or listen to what God is telling her without fear of what her peers think of her. Worship is also an awesome outreach tool. We watch how nonbelievers look at a kid in love with Jesus who is worshiping—they know that there is something special there, and they want it."

Sunday mornings and Thursday-night Bible studies are geared to be more intimate. They focus on relationship building and getting into the Word.

They do three trips a year: Winter Camp, Mexico Outreach during spring break, and a Houseboat trip. They always do their own trips, handling all the details from bringing in a speaker who they think will connect to their kids' needs to choosing a good worship band. They even do their own food and do it well. They find that they can control the intimacy and the flow a whole lot better when they are in control of these variables since they are the ones who know their kids.

The Rock claims to be first and foremost a student-led ministry. "Our church kids, particularly our leadership kids, understand our ministry because we go through it with them, and they play a huge role in the ministry, making sure that visitors feel welcome and safe. They know what our ministry is about and have bought into the program. They've seen it work and have been blessed by it."

They rely heavily on leadership kids to attract the unchurched kids in their classes. "Kids talk and have more influence on their peers than any adult could. They want to be where the babes are. And it's a good excuse not to sit around at home and listen to Mom and Dad fight."

Thanksgiving Baskets

Rick worked in my office. He runs programs for urban kids who live in poor, run-down apartment complexes. He has a huge heart for people hurting financially. Rick also runs an outreach at the local city college. College students come to activities and hear about the Word of God, sometimes for the first time.

Rick noticed that a large group of people attending the college were in poor financial situations. He talked to the administration and found there were a large number of single mothers and young families on governmental support. Rick asked permission to help and acquired a list of needy people at the school.

Rick contacted several local churches. Each church put together a team of people during the month of November. These teams put together Thanksgiving baskets for every person on that list—turkeys, canned foods, rice, pasta, a whole assortment of goodies. The people from the churches came on campus and distributed the baskets to the needy people.

Now this list is growing, and so is the opportunity for ministry. Churches are connecting with needy people all over the city. And people all over the city are learning that the church cares.

Campus Life at Granite Bay High School in California (a high school campus outreach ministry)

Rob runs a campus outreach for Youth for Christ/Campus Life, targeting unchurched kids on a high school campus.

Rob's typical week starts on Monday at lunchtime when he visits the campus and sees students during both lunch periods. "I roam and introduce myself to friends of the students I already know. Generally I'll say, 'Hi, I'm Rob I'm John's probation officer—what's your name?' First of all, John cracks up and then all his friends look at John like 'We never knew you got into that much trouble.' It breaks the ice, we have a laugh, and then I tell them who I really am and share about what we're doing that night or upcoming trips and events."

In between the two lunches Rob will have lunch with a senior student or two who has a flexible schedule and simply listen to their lives and field any questions they may have. Rob meets with several students after school each week, as well as occasional meetings with core kids.

Monday night is their outreach event at the local community center. A core group of students get there early and help set up, preparing for the students. The Campus Life meetings are generally topical and revolve around real-life issues. Students will welcome the group, introduce visitors, and generally lead the first game or mixer. A few mixers, a game or two, video highlights from the previous week's events, and then a discussion starter. Rob usually speaks for no more than five to 10 minutes, then breaks the group up into smaller groups. Ideally the questions have been e-mailed to the volunteers earlier, and they have already thought through their personal answers. They wrap it up with a general Q&A time, and small group representatives will share their findings.

Content is very relational in nature. A number of times a year the gospel is presented using stories and some of Jesus' parables. On occasion an invitation is given, and generally some form of response card is used for follow-up purposes. Occasionally it is left up to the student to seek out a staff person. Regardless of the format, "Most club weeks our faith is discussed in one manner or another. Sometimes it's as simple as 'You know we're a Christian organization, and we're here because we really care about you.' But each week our staff are seeking one-on-one time with students where we are building relationships and sharing our faith with them."

After Campus Life, more than 90 percent of the students and all the volunteers proceed to the local eatery. They simply hang out, meet new kids, and learn a little more about first-time visitors. This is when the real ministry takes place. Students will ask for private time and go for a walk and share what's happening in their lives. Multiple decisions for Christ have been made on the way home on Monday evenings.

Aside from Rob's presence, Campus Life is primarily advertised by the student leaders who invite friends and hand out fliers. Rob advertises all trips and upcoming events in the school newspaper. Last year they formally became an on-campus club at the high school. They have a faculty advisor and a real campus presence. The on-campus club needs to be student run. It gives the ministry great exposure and the ability to advertise to the general school population.

You'll almost always see Rob and his two boys (ages 7 and 9) at the Thursday-evening freshmen football games. "My own children are the best tools for meeting new kids. Last week we played catch in the stands and included six to eight students we really didn't know. Games are a great place to meet kids. Kids like to see me there, and it gives me an excuse to call several key kids and tell them what a great job they did."

Hot Cocoa

Jason is a youth pastor at an Assembly of God church in the Sacramento area. Jason had the desire to reach the school campuses around him. He hired several interns and assigned each intern to a specific campus with the following task: Serve this campus with no ulterior motives.

The interns introduced themselves to the principals of the given campuses. They explained that they worked for a church, but their job was to serve the school. Name it: scrape gum off bleachers, pick up trash, be an extra yard duty person—whatever the need.

Some principals were more skeptical than others, yet the interns were put to work. Some were given specific jobs; others were allowed to come and be a positive presence on campus.

One cold December day, one of the interns, who worked on a pretty rough campus, brought a huge pot full of hot cocoa. He set up a table at the front of the school and handed out hot cocoa. As kids arrived, stepped out of cars, unloaded from the buses, they were greeted with a warm cup of cocoa. There were no Bible verses printed on the cups, no fliers handed out with the napkins—just hot cocoa.

The principal saw the intern walking around later that day, and he quickly flagged him down.

"Jim! Jim, I need to talk to you." The intern, feeling a little nervous, approached the principal, who seemed to be choosing his words carefully. "Jim, I don't know what your motive was for the hot cocoa, but I want you to know that you have changed the atmosphere on this campus today. I haven't seen the kids act like this before. I can't explain it, but they all were smiling, and they all had a cup of hot cocoa."

Friendship Evangelism

For the last decade, the primary source of evangelism at Saddleback Church's junior high ministry is simply friends telling friends and bringing them to church.

Kurt Johnston, junior high pastor of Saddleback Church in Lake Forest, California, calls this friendship evangelism: Students living an authentic life and sharing Jesus with their unchurched friends. Students who commit to friendship evangelism basically follow a three-step strategy:

1. Act like a Christian, live an authentic life, be who you say you are.

2. Begin to pray for opportunities to share your faith.

3. Communicate with love.

Kurt and his staff consistently remind them of this in their small groups and occasionally they teach a weekend series on the subject.

The weekend program probably serves as a place for students to invite their friends. This program is the junior high ministry's most evangelistic, ongoing program, but it's really just a seeker-friendly worship service.

The weekend program agenda is simple. They start with fun and fast music. Then they have a game or a video. More music and more games or videos. Then they have a student share his or her testimony. A little more worship music, followed by the message. This program is located at the church in a large, semipermanent tent. They have about five churched students for every unchurched student.

Although friendship evangelism is this junior high ministry's primary evangelism method, it is not their only method. Saddleback offers a couple of events a year that focus on evangelism. These might be renting out a local water park where a couple thousand kids will show up, an annual summer camp, or their new low-budget student center/coffee house. Kurt maintains that "Our strategy is to provide real, relevant, relational, and relaxed programs that support our students' efforts. The deal we make with students is basically, 'You go out on a limb and share Christ and invite a friend to church, and we'll make sure the limb doesn't break out from under you. We'll make you proud you took the chance!'"

Although Kurt believes these adult-run programs are great, he still thinks friendship evangelism is where it's at. "The reason I believe so strongly in friendship evangelism, as flawed as it is, is because I think big, ongoing outreach programs handicap our students in the long run. I don't want them to rely on me, the church, our budget, our facilities, etc., to reach their friends. I want them to see early on that a program doesn't change a life, but a relationship does. If a kid leaves Saddleback and goes to a tiny little church in the Midwest with two students and no outreach program, I want that student to have the understanding that *he* is the outreach program. It may not click right now while they're in a big, happening environment, but I'm hoping we're planting seeds of maturity in their hearts that will reap results when it matters most."

Saddleback doesn't do typical "campus ministry"—in other words, clubs, outreaches, etc. But they do minister to campuses by having interns who are responsible for a particular campus, show up at events, take those kids to lunch—whatever it takes. Their strategy isn't for these interns to run programs but to be support for kids as they attempt to be a light.

Kurt admits, "I'm sure we don't see as many conversions each year, and our attendance isn't as high as it could be if we did more proactive outreach program, but I think that when friends reach friends, their decisions are more apt to stick for the long haul. Idealistic? Totally! Effective? Somewhat. Healthy? Boy, I hope so. The best way? No way!"

Crossover Basketball League

It's Thursday afternoon in the small, dilapidated, inner-city junior high school gym, and the bell rang a half-hour ago. There are no school leagues playing today, but the gym is full of kids with one desire: basketball!

The Crossover Basketball League is a program for "at risk" youth that places Christian coaches in the lives of young boys. Many of these boys are fatherless, and most of them struggle in school. The school sports leagues require a certain GPA to play; Crossover only requires the boys to commit to attendance. Each boy gets game time, regardless of skill.

It's no surprise that several hundred students have signed up for Crossover Basketball League this year, leaving a huge number of kids on a waiting list. "It's a great problem to have," says Crossover Director Omar Turner. "They don't have much in common, but they all love basketball."

What better way to provide love and support to an unchurched generation searching for meaning, a generation of youth that lacks positive role models—or any adults for that matter—who are willing to notice them or devote any time to them? And Crossover opens doors to greater things. Each practice contains a 15-minute "huddle group" where coaches lead discussions on subjects like integrity, character, and friendship. Many of these discussions open doors to conversations about God.

Students hear more about what a relationship with God is like at Crossover's monthly "faith" events. This voluntary component of the league usually attracts over 90 percent of the students to a fun event where the gospel is shared.

Crossover is an effective way to not only put positive role models in the lives of kids, but also to share the gospel with a godless generation. Working hand in hand with the schools, Crossover respects the lines that schools set. Don Talley, the developer of Crossover's structure, incorporated three very separate components to effectively reach the unchurched teenager. Those components are: the athletic component, the personal development component, and the faith component. The faith component is completely optional. Coaches don't "preach" at the on-campus practices. They do, however, have many opportunities to share with the students with whom they have built relationships both off campus and at the faith events.

The personal development content is a 12-week small group curriculum written to help the students develop greater character, confidence, and responsibility. The two large group events spread out during the 12 weeks are designed to give the students opportunities to understand the gospel. Usually a speaker, pastor, or one of the coaches will give their testimony.

Feeding the Football Team

My buddy Leonard has a small church in North Highlands, a suburb of Sacramento. His church meets at a local high school and reaches families in the area. One of Leonard's attendees is a coach for the school's football team. The coach was talking to Leonard about how they used to get the team together for dinner before the games. But parent participation wasn't as high as it used to be, and the whole dinner idea had been benched for a while.

Leonard jumped at this opportunity. The church got a group of volunteers together—"Let's do dinner!" And a hungry football team wouldn't decline a free meal. Now before every home game, the church feeds the entire football team and coaching staff. The kids are getting to know Leonard, the pastor, as well as other members of the congregation.

No preaching, no mandatory messages—just dinner.

Now more doors are being opened. Football players are interested in the church that's feeding them. Relationships are developing between players and church volunteers. And Leonard is now asked to offer words of encouragement and even a prayer before each game.

Insight

Does small town mean small numbers? Not necessarily.

Paradise, California, is a small, one-high-school town in Northern California. Everyone knows everyone, and the youth groups are small—well, most of them.

Paradise Alliance Church has up to 300 kids a week coming on Sunday mornings. I didn't believe it until I saw it myself when I went there to speak. They meet Sunday mornings in the gym. Youth Director Tim Bolin says, "Here in Paradise, Sunday a.m. works for people. We meet at the second service, so it's not so early that kids can't get up and come."

Nothing special about the agenda: music, a crowdbreaker or two, then a message. This is a time where students can come and socialize before and after. "They hear great music, have fun interacting with people, and hear a message of hope and grace."

Students are the key to inviting other students. Tim says, "Our students take ownership in the event and programs and then will bring their friends to come and check it out. One student who has a sense of ownership is better than 1,000 fliers! Provide an event that looks, smells, and *is* attractive."

During the week Paradise uses small groups. In this format, each student has the opportunity to investigate the Bible and ask questions safely. Building relationships is key.

Paradise also does a big, first-of-the-year kickoff at the church facility—three nights of extreme games, crowd breakers, speakers, and food. They work with other churches in town to reach kids for Christ through this outreach.

The Note

Ken works in a small town in Michigan. He runs an outreach program there reaching kids on multiple campuses and getting them involved in the local church.

One Saturday, after weeks of nonstop, 60- to 70-hour weeks, he had a day off. He made sure not to schedule anything on this day so he could just catch up with the many fix-it jobs that were in dire need around his house. Ken was a pretty handy guy. Living on a limited income, he fixed most things around the house himself, including his cars.

After breakfast on this particular morning, he looked out his front window while sipping his coffee. Parked on the street in front of his house was a large old vehicle with its hood open and a Latino man standing over the engine, fidgeting with the carburetor.

Ken's city had been having problems with the white population getting along with a newer Latino population. Ken had been an advocate of reconciliation for the community and had promoted acceptance of what some people called a bothersome group of people that were making their living picking vegetables.

Ken quickly stepped away from the window, hoping the man had not seen him. Ken wasn't about to waste his cherished Saturday. He tried to start a few chores, but he found himself peeking out the front window. The man was still there. The car was still there.

Angry, Ken prayed, *Okay Jesus! Am I supposed to bag my Saturday and go help this guy?* Ken thought. *Is this the guy that you were talking about when you said love thy neighbor?* Ken was bummed that he had even thought of that passage or that the passage came to mind so fast after asking God that first question.

Unable to work, Ken gave up the battle. *Okay, Jesus, I'll do it!*

Ken went outside and introduced himself to the man. He didn't speak any English whatsoever; he just rattled off a couple words in Spanish that Ken didn't understand. Ken pointed at the engine and the man started talking again, seemingly frustrated, throwing his hands over his head.

Ken gave his best effort to communicate that he was going to try to help. The man seemed agreeable, so Ken got to work assessing the problem.

Ken spent the entire morning fixing the man's car, including a few runs to the auto parts store. When the car finally started, the man smiled from ear to ear and talked without stopping. Ken didn't understand a word he was saying, but he understood perfectly.

Ken got back to his Saturday and finished numerous projects, feeling great about his accomplishments when he finally went to bed.

The next day when Ken's family came home from church, they noticed something on the front porch. After Ken parked, he walked to the front of the house to find a basket of fruit sitting on the porch. There was a note. Ken picked up the basket and opened the note. The words almost made him drop the basket: *thank you so very much.* And it was signed—*Jesus.*

Ken had heard the Spanish name, pronounced "Hey Seuss," many times. He knew it was a popular name in the Latino population. But Ken couldn't help but think, "Whatever you've done to the least of my brethren, you've done it to me."

No matter which way you look at it, Ken did it for Jesus, and Jesus was grateful.

Meeting Needs

All of the above stories are true, and all have one thing in common—acts of service. These people all saw a physical need and met it.

In John, chapter 2, Jesus does his first miracle. He doesn't preach. He doesn't even say, "Repent, the kingdom of heaven is here!" (a message he often preached). He met a physical need. Everywhere Jesus went, he met physical needs. Matthew 4:23 reads: "Jesus went throughout Galilee, teaching in their synagogues, preaching the good news of the kingdom, and healing every disease and sickness among the people."

Evangelism is much more than just a presentation. Evangelism is intentional, and it's an action. This takes more work and, often, more money. But this kind of evangelism isn't about what we say—it's who we are. And who we are will speak louder than anything we say and often give us opportunities to share our faith.

Initiating Outreach to the Unchurched

**You've read the book—
now what?**

From the beginning of this book, we've talked about understanding and reaching the unchurched. We've taken a peek into the mind of today's unchurched students, we examined different methods to reach them, and we've even done a self-evaluation about our outlook and our own faith.

Now the ball is in your court. You've read the book—now what?

I think that describes my mind-set when my friend Rich challenged me with his snowblower story in the last chapter. It was a powerful story, but so what?

I went home and told Rich's story about reaching out to his neighbors to my wife, Lori. My heart was troubled. I thought of my next-door neighbors on both sides. I was embarrassed to admit I'd never really thought about talking with them about Christ or inviting them to church. I hadn't even considered inviting them over for dinner. Some minister of evangelism, huh?

"This is my job!" I barked at my wife. "Why am I not even reaching my neighbor?"

Lori and I prayed that night. We prayed that God would use us. We prayed that God would help us to "be intentional" at reaching our unchurched neighbors.

We recently moved to a new street with 12 houses, all new residents. Every time I saw a neighbor on the street, God tugged at my heart. Lori and I wanted to make an impact on our street, so we tried to meet as many of our neighbors as possible. We said hi to some as they passed our house walking their dogs. Others we saw at the mailbox. But in the age of automatic garage door openers and six-foot fences, there were neighbors we never even saw.

Christmas rolled around, and we decided to do something intentional. We threw a Christmas party for all the neighbors on our street. We had no plans to set up an easel and draw two cliffs with the word "sin" written in a chasm below. We had no agenda other than meeting our neighbors and hosting a fun dessert.

That afternoon they started arriving one family at a time. But before long, kids I'd just met were running loose in the house, and neighbors who had barely given more than a quick wave to each other were talking and laughing over veggie trays and Christmas cookies. An hour after the party started, we had nine of our twelve neighbor families in our living room.

I had several people ask me what I do for a living. I told them I worked with students as a youth minister. Some got quiet when I said the word *minister*. Others asked questions about what church I attended.

A single mom from down the street asked if I attended a local church. I told her I did as we watched our kids playing together on my stairway. She said, "You know, my kids really need something like church." The conversation continued, and I invited her and her kids to our Christmas Eve service.

So on Christmas Eve my family sat in church with a single mom, her boyfriend, and her two kids. And they heard the gospel. Why? A simple party. We didn't preach, we didn't hand out tracts, we didn't set up the flannel board in the living room. We didn't even play chubby bunnies. We laughed and talked and opened the door to future relationships and future conversations.

Reaching the unchurched—whether they're our neighbors next door or teenagers at the local school—comes down to one simple word: *love*.